CONSTITUTIONAL CONSCIENCE

H. JEFFERSON POWELL

Constitutional Conscience

The Moral Dimension of Judicial Decision

THE UNIVERSITY OF CHICAGO PRESS ⤆

CHICAGO AND LONDON

KF 8700
.P69
2008

H. JEFFERSON POWELL is a professor at the Duke University School of Law and the author of *The Moral Tradition of American Constitutionalism* and *A Community Built on Words: The Constitution in History and Politics,* the latter published by the University of Chicago Press.

The University of Chicago Press, Chicago 60637
The University of Chicago Press, Ltd., London
© 2008 by The University of Chicago
All rights reserved. Published 2008
Printed in the United States of America

17 16 15 14 13 12 11 10 09 08   1 2 3 4 5

Portions of chapter 4 originally appeared in H. Jefferson Powell, Constitutional Virtues, 9 Green Bag 2d 379 (2006). © 2006 The Green Bag, Inc. Reprinted by permission of The Green Bag.

ISBN-13: 978-0-226-67725-5 (cloth)
ISBN-10: 0-226-67725-7 (cloth)

Library of Congress Cataloging-in-Publication Data
Powell, Jefferson, 1954–
  Constitutional conscience : the moral dimension of judicial decision / H. Jefferson Powell.
    p. cm.
  Includes bibliographical references and index.
  ISBN-13: 978-0-226-67725-5 (cloth : alk. paper)
  ISBN-10: 0-226-67725-7 (cloth : alk. paper) 1. Judicial process—United States. 2. Justice, Administration of—United States. 3. Judges—United States. 4. Judicial discretion—United States. 5. Constitutional law—United States. I. Title.
  KF8700.P69 2008
  347.73'2634—dc22
                                                                    2007032536

♾ The paper used in this publication meets the minimum requirements of the American National Standard for Information Sciences— Permanence of Paper for Printed Library Materials, ANSI Z39.48-1992.

For Sarah, with love
. . . our little book

CONTENTS

PREFACE

In many law schools in the United States, constitutional law is a required first-year course. The wisdom of that curricular decision is at least debatable, for regardless of the instructor's intentions, an introductory course in the law of the United States Constitution can easily turn into a sustained lesson in cynicism. Constitutional law, at least much of the time, deals with matters that are clearly of political import, but the language in which we discuss it generally sounds like a form of apolitical law. The justices of the Supreme Court, whose opinions make up the core of most introductory courses, sometimes accuse one another of willful blindness to the Constitution's commands while insisting that their own views are the product of a scrupulous fidelity to those same commands, and it takes little time for the student to realize that the justices' positions generally fall into patterns, both in terms of outcomes and of alliance within the Court, that seem best explained as ideological. It is hardly surprising that some students come to the despairing conclusion that constitutional law is a systematic hypocrisy, and that others happily embrace the same understanding of the law because it seems the product of hard-bitten realism.

I do not believe that constitutional law is, or ought to be, or needs to be, an exercise in hypocrisy. If we (students, their teachers, lawyers, judges, citizens) become cynics about the law of the Constitution, then of course we can make the language of the law hypocritical, and if enough of us do that for long enough, then constitutional law will be a fraud. But that is a choice that we need not make. It is possible to understand the American constitutional tradition in a different light, as an always fallible, often flawed effort to do what its language implies it to be: the faithful interpretation of a fundamental law that is this republic's chosen means of self-governance. How we can believe that to be so in the face of all the evidence to the contrary is the theme of what follows.

←

The debts I have incurred in thinking and writing about this subject go back over many years, and I know I cannot acknowledge them adequately. I want to mention, however, a few specific contributions. Over the years, my own first-year students have been a challenge and an inspiration, and much that is here is the product of our efforts together to understand constitutional law. Much of chapter 4 has its origins in the Sixth Annual Walter F. Murphy Lecture in American Constitutionalism delivered under the auspices of the James Madison Program in American Ideals and Institutions at Princeton University. It was an honor to be invited to deliver the lecture, and to participate in the lively discussion that followed. I am deeply grateful to Joseph Vining, who gave the first draft of the manuscript an extraordinarily close, charitable, and critical reading. I greatly appreciate as well the advice and encouragement that David Lange, Robert Mosteller, Jedediah Purdy, and James Boyd White each gave me at important points. As always, my daughter Sara has provided interest, enthusiasm, and insight. I am indebted as well to John Tryneski for his keen editorial skills, to Erik Carlson for his excellent copyedit of the manuscript, and to the Press's anonymous readers for their comments.

Finally, this little book would not exist except for the numberless conversations I have had about its themes with Sarah Sharp. To those conversations, Sarah brought both her deep moral passion and her keen lawyer's mind, and I have learned more than I can say from her. I hope she will accept the book and its dedication as a sign of our new life together.

INTRODUCTION

Near the end of his opinion in *Marbury v. Madison*, Chief Justice John Marshall made an interesting suggestion. His topic, at that point in the opinion, was the justification he claimed for the judiciary's exercising the authority to disregard a statutory command when, in the judges' opinion, that command contravenes the Constitution of the United States. Having rested his claim primarily on the nature of a written constitution and the necessities of judicial decision, Marshall added, as an ancillary consideration, the import of the third paragraph of Article VI, which provides that all legislators and executive and "judicial Officers, both of the United States and of the several States, shall be bound by Oath or Affirmation, to support this Constitution." This requirement, Marshall asserted, was evidence that "the framers of the constitution contemplated that instrument, as a rule for the government of courts"—and thus that the courts so governed were empowered to follow the Constitution instead of Congress in the event of conflict, to exercise (in modern language) the power of judicial review:[1]

> Why otherwise does it direct the judges to take an oath to support it? This oath certainly applies, in an especial manner, to their conduct in their official character. How immoral to impose it on them, if they were to be used as the instruments, and the knowing instruments, for violating what they swear to support?
>
> The oath of office, too, imposed by the legislature, is completely demonstrative of the legislative opinion on this subject. It is in these words, "I do solemnly swear

that I will administer justice without respect to persons, and do equal right to the poor and to the rich; and that I will faithfully and impartially discharge all the duties incumbent on me as according to the best of my abilities and understanding, agreeably to the constitution, and laws of the United States."

Why does a judge swear to discharge his duties agreeably to the constitution of the United States, if that constitution forms no rule for his government? If it is closed upon him, and cannot be inspected by him?

If such be the real state of things, this is worse than solemn mockery. To prescribe, or to take this oath, becomes equally a crime.[2]

Marshall's attempt to support judicial review, even in part, by invoking the Constitution's oath requirement has not fared well among modern scholars, who argue that it begs the real question raised by judicial disregard of a statute (Whose understanding of the Constitution is to prevail, the judges' or Congress's?), or even that the oath requirement actually undercuts Marshall's overall reasoning.[3]

The canon of interpretive charity counsels us to look not so much for the holes we can poke in Marshall's comments as for some sense of why he thought them worth making.[4] Marshall's language clearly suggests that he did not see his discussion of the oath requirement as a lightweight or throwaway argument: the requirement, he insisted, would become "immoral . . . worse than solemn mockery . . . a crime," if judges were obliged in their decisions to follow statutory rules that contradicted what they believed were the commands of the Constitution. This is strong, emotive language, and even if we cannot be sure of Marshall's precise line of thought, I believe that we can discern the general thrust of his words. Marshall believed that the practice of judicial review rests not only on the structural features of the American Constitution that he emphasized earlier in his opinion—the political "theory . . . essentially attached to a written constitution" and its relationship to the judicial office[5]—but flows as well from the judge's individual obligations as a moral actor. He perceived in the oath requirement a juxtaposition of the judiciary's governmental role and the judge's personal conscience, one that gives moral weight to the individual's exercise of the power of judicial review that the community has entrusted to him.[6]

This implies, in turn, that a judge must take the Constitution—the Constitution itself, the interpretable document that is open to the judge's own "inspection" in the search for its meaning and application—as the ultimate rule governing his official actions. To accept this conclusion is not to decide in advance that the judiciary is the exclusive or (always) the final ordinary interpreter of the Constitution, or that an individual judge is always entitled to follow his own rather than someone else's conscientious view of the Constitution's meaning. (Marshall thought that some constitutional questions were "political" in nature and answerable only by one of the nonjudicial branches of government, and he doubted neither the normative weight of practice and precedent nor the duty of a lower-court judge to obey a superior tribunal.)[7] But Marshall's fierce insistence that judicial review is in some manner a question of, or for, the judge's conscience implies a closer connection than is sometimes acknowledged between how we understand constitutional law and how individual judges understand the moral circumstances in which they carry out their duties. For Marshall, the judicial oath is not, as some of his critics contend, "merely an affirmation of loyalty to the political principles of the nation, [rather than] a promise to judge in a certain way or ways."[8] Instead, it bears directly on how the judge carries out his duties and understands his role in relationship to other governmental officials.

One hundred ninety-nine years after John Marshall wrote *Marbury v. Madison*, one of his most distinguished twenty-first-century colleagues on the federal bench, Richard A. Posner, made a comment in a law review article that is, at first glance anyway, startling. Judge Posner's intent was to rebut the possible charge that his professional beau ideal, "a good pragmatist judge," would simply ignore the value of "maintain[ing] continuity with established understandings of the law" in his or her search for the best social outcome in a case. Not so, Posner reassured his readers: the pragmatist judge will give full weight to the costs in terms of "uncertainty about legal obligation and . . . cynicism about the judicial process" that unguarded judicial creativity risks. In doing so, however, Posner hastened to disavow a moral reading of his words: "The point is not that the judge has some kind of moral or even political duty to abide by constitutional or statutory text, or by precedent; that would be formalism."[9] Let us put to one side for the moment Posner's assumption that "that would be formalism" is sufficient to condemn an argument about the actions of judges (the issue, though not Posner's views on it, will return),[10] and also the views of statutory construction and stare decisis that his comment implies: I want to focus on his belief, which I shall now put in the form of an assertion rather than a denial, that a judge has no kind of moral or even political duty to abide by constitutional text.

On the face of it, this assertion stands in direct contradiction to Chief Justice Marshall's discussion of the oath in *Marbury*. The 1803 opinion appears to rest the legitimacy of judicial review, in part, on the judge's moral duty to "inspect" the Constitution—surely assumed here as earlier in the opinion to be the written and formally adopted instrument—and accept its commands as the supreme rule of government for judicial action that overrides contrary rules promulgated by Congress. The 2002 article appears to dismiss entirely any link between the judge's moral and political duties (if any) and the written Constitution by expressly assuming that courts should continue to engage in judicial review. The contrast is quite remarkable: *Marbury v. Madison* is, for all the sniping it takes from scholars, *the* canonical enunciation of the power of judicial review in modern American law, and almost all American constitutionalists, now as in Marshall's day, have treated the authority of the Constitution's text as axiomatic.[11] For a sitting federal judge to repudiate both in one fell swoop—without the sky falling, or at least questions being raised about his fitness for office[12]—strongly suggests that it is time to reexamine the validity of Chief Justice Marshall's assumption that the Constitution, judicial review, and the moral duties of the federal judge are closely linked.

Judge Posner himself has acknowledged the profound issues his 2002 remark raises, without immediate reference to *Marbury*, to be sure, and proposed an answer to the suggestion that his view "counsel[s] disobedience to the oath that Article VI . . . requires":

> This would be so if the oath were interpreted to require obeisance to specific text or precedents, but that would be ridiculous, since precedents are overruled and the text of the Constitution has frequently been rewritten by the Supreme Court in the guise of interpretation. The oath is a loyalty oath rather than a direction concerning judicial discretion. The loyalty demanded is to the United States, its form of government, and its accepted official practices, which include loose judicial interpretation of the constitutional text.[13]

It is wrong, Posner claims, to accuse him of "seem[ing] to make the oath a kind of lark."[14] The constitutional oath pledges those who take it to loyalty to "the accepted official practices" of American government. But Posner clearly does not include among those practices a sense of moral obligation to obey the Constitution's text. Despite his reference to "loose . . . interpretation of the constitutional text" (which might imply in a different context that something resembling interpretation of a document is going on), nothing in the tone of this passage (no "*obeisance* to *specific text*"; the Supreme Court "rewrites" the text "in the guise of interpretation") gives us any reason to think that Posner has rethought his earlier assertion that a judge has no kind of moral or even political duty to abide by constitutional text. Indeed, what he discounted earlier as "formalism" he subsequently dismisses as "ridiculous."

Judge Posner's new formulation sharpens his disagreement with *Marbury*: Posner has expressly adopted the "loyalty test" view of the oath that *Marbury* contradicts, and he now appears to concede that his approach *does* counsel violation of the oath of office if that oath is thought to require adherence to the "specific text" that Marshall wanted judges to interpret. Of course, in itself this disagreement proves nothing, other than Posner's willingness to stake out a position that renders him open to attack from many sides (and that of course can be a sign of the virtue of intellectual courage): perhaps Marshall was wrong and Posner is right.[15] And important as both judges are in the history of American law, my interest in them in this book lies not in resolving their relationship but in the issue their apparent disagreement lays bare.

Let me briefly state the two premises of this book. The first is that in discussing constitutional law we can propose, for public consideration, moral or ethical evaluations meaningfully, if minimally. The issue of how to think about such propositions in a culture such as ours is incredibly difficult, and it will emerge as a central theme of this book. For now, all that I need to ask the reader to entertain is a very thin set of ethical presuppositions. It is generally wrong for human beings, acting as participants in a community or society, to lie about their actions or intentions. There is, as a consequence, a moral difference between making a mistake in acting in relationship to a community or society and acting deceitfully or in bad faith. This difference is especially weighty when the individual is acting for the community—we speak of someone holding an office or position of trust, a phrase that underlines the implicit moral significance of her relationship to the community.[16] Good faith in acting for a community is a necessity if the community is to function successfully, and the community therefore has a moral claim on the person who undertakes to act on its behalf. (We will not stop to consider the possibility that a society can be so morally repugnant that it can make no such claim even on individuals who purport to act on its behalf.) For some people, this moral claim begins and ends with the value to the community of good-faith action. I think it more congruent with our experience of such matters to see this moral claim as a internal demand about how I should act, even if the demand is triggered by the needs of others. But this is a dispute we need not resolve: the main line of reasoning is one that was familiar to the founding generation and is equally so to twenty-first-century Americans.[17] For anyone who sincerely disagrees with it, I have nothing (in this work) to say. I shall assume, instead, that it makes sense generally in American society to speak of honesty and good faith in dealing with and on behalf of the American political community.

My second premise is that constitutional law's central function is to provide a means of resolving political conflict that accepts the inevitability and persistence of such conflict rather than the possibility of consensus or even broad agreement on many issues. The best statement I know of this assumption was set forth several years ago by the philosopher Stuart Hampshire in a series of lectures entitled Justice Is Conflict. In a complex, heterogeneous society such as the United States, Hampshire argued, moral disagreement over a wide range of social issues is inescapable: political conflict is thus a feature of any free or open society. At the same time, any society must have means for resolving particular controversies, and for those means to serve their social function of conflict resolution they must observe what Hampshire asserted to be the universal claim of procedural justice or fairness that both sides to a controversy will be heard. But procedural justice is never found, outside the theorist's study, in a pure state of abstract rationality: in any given society it will be embedded in "the customary and rule-governed procedures of public argument and decision making appropriate to such cases in this particular society." Even though the "[p]rocedures of conflict resolution within any state are always being criticized and are always changing and are never as fair and as unbiased as they ideally might be," they can play the role of settling controversies because they are "well known and part of a continuous history." Widespread disregard for these society-specific traditions would undermine—in the end, fatally—their general acceptability as a means of restoring or maintaining social peace: "The institutions and their rituals hold society together, insofar as they are successful and well established in the resolution of moral and political conflicts according to particular local and national conventions."[18]

It is immaterial to the argument of this book whether Hampshire was right in making assertions about all complex societies. Whatever the truth of his universal claims, his argument describes American constitutional law from a useful perspective. Constitutional law is one of the central institutions for conflict resolution in this society; as a formal matter it is, within its substantive boundaries, the most central ("the supreme Law of the Land," as Article VI puts it). Despite the fact that with some frequency particular constitutional decisions (the school desegregation decisions, *Roe v. Wade*, warrantless surveillance in the wake of 9/11) anger this or that part of the American populace, as a general matter it seems clear that most Americans see the overall system of constitutional decision making as legitimate, and despite the constant existence of gaps between constitutional principle and political practice, to a remarkable extent both elected officials and public opinion accept Supreme Court decisions as binding. There can be little doubt, I think, that this is because constitutional argument and Court decisions are "well known and part of the continuous history" of the Republic.

The substantive features of constitutional law, moreover, track Hampshire's analysis.[19] The power of judicial review itself, as *Marbury v. Madison* itself stated, rests on the duty of the federal courts to resolve "Cases and Controversies" in circumstances and between contending parties over whom the courts have jurisdiction. Not all constitutional decisions, to be sure, involve a controversy between different parties. An executive-branch lawyer giving advice to the president about the constitutionality of a certain course of action usually does not do so after the fact, when individuals or institutions are ranged against one another over the results of some action, but in advance of the president's decision: the controversy in that case is conceptual, a matter of weighing the arguments for and against the proposed decision. In both situations, however, long-established practices of argument and reasoning identify how it is that the constitutional decision maker—whether a judge rendering judgment, a lawyer offering advice, or an elected official making a political determination—is to go about coming to a decision about whatever constitutional issues may be in question, and therefore resolving the interpersonal, institutional, or intellectual conflict. The forms of constitutional argument, the sorts of considerations that a constitutional decision maker can take into account in coming to a decision, are to be found in our actual, traditional practices of constitutional interpretation. A substantial divergence between what constitutional decision makers say they are doing and what they actually are or are perceived to be doing would undermine in the long term the value of constitutional law to American society.[20] Again, if this last assumption seems wrong or wildly implausible to the reader, this book will not attempt to persuade him or her otherwise.

So much for premises: what remains for this introduction is a statement of what I shall argue on their basis. The central claim of this book is that Chief Justice Marshall was right to believe that the exercise of the power of judicial review presents profound moral questions for those who wield it and thus for all of us affected by it. As my contrast between Marshall and Judge Posner is meant to illustrate, this claim is controversial. Posner's view of law as a morally neutral tool for the achievement of goals set by wholly extralegal considerations is widely shared, and not just by those who share his interest in understanding law through the lens of economics. From that perspective, talk about the moral dimension of constitutional interpretation is pointless, because such conversations are in principle irresolvable, expressions of conflicting preferences none of which can be said to be right or wrong, better or worse, unless they are translated into other terms, such as efficiency or social order, at which point they are (it is assumed) no longer moral.[21] A surprisingly similar position in practice is that maintained by those who insist that constitutional questions always and simply involve choices between substantive moral values. Like the Posnerian, such proponents of constitutional law as morality treat constitutional language itself as empty, a mere tool for advancing other ends than those the language purports to address. In doing so, they leave no basis in constitutional law itself for conversation with those who hold opposing moral commitments.[22]

However widespread, these understandings of constitutional decision making are, I believe, misleading. Our actual practices of interpreting the Constitution presuppose the existence of a moral dimension to those practices: put another way, much of what we say and do in constitutional interpretation is meaningless—a "solemn mockery" indeed—if constitutional decision is in fact free of the sort of moral commitment that Marshall invoked in his opinion in *Marbury*. Marshall portrayed the constitutional judge's task as defined by the moral obligation encapsulated in his oath of office, and that obligation was not to reach decisions on some ethical basis found outside the Constitution but rather to decide on the basis of the Constitution. The American constitutional tradition has followed Marshall: to this day, constitutional-law argument consists of sentences such as "The due process clause requires X" and "We therefore must conclude Y." Whether he wishes to or not, in deciding a constitutional case, even the most instrumentalist judge necessarily keeps faith with, or is faithless to, the assumptions reflected in the language that he or she has inherited. With the introduction of good (and bad) faith as elements in constitutional law, we clearly have entered the realm of moral obligation to which Marshall appealed in his discussion of the judicial oath.[23] I shall argue that we should follow Marshall in this regard and strive to be more self-conscious about the moral circumstances of judicial review.

The key to understanding the moral dimension of constitutional decision, I shall argue, is the demand it places on the conscience of the judge. In almost every controversial decision, the judge will confront interpretive choices, many of which have multiple resolutions that can be justified by craftsmanlike arguments. There is no external metric by which such choices can be made that will allow a noninstrumentalist judge to escape the need to decide what seems most persuasive among two or more plausible alternatives, and no algorithm that will resolve for her the conflicting claims of plausibility. She can act in accordance with the language and ideals of our traditional practices only by deciding in good faith, according to her conscience. Much of this book, therefore, explores what it means to have a good (or bad) conscience in constitutional decision making.

As I have already claimed, American constitutional law has a distinct identity: only some sorts of assertions "count" as constitutional arguments. But as I shall discuss at some length, the sheerly instrumentalist judge can use constitutional language without respecting that identity. In contrast, a judge acting out of a constitutional conscience will use the language fairly: working from the assumption that we can discuss constitutional issues in meaningful debate and not simply engage in a shouting match over irresolvable differences, she will make the arguments to herself and others with candor, including an overt recognition of the ambiguities and uncertainties present in the Constitution's text and in any resolution of many constitutional issues; with honesty about the fact that constitutional decision making is a creative endeavor, involving the creation of new law and not just obedience to existing law; and with a certain kind of humility about the limits of constitutional adjudication. I call the habit of exhibiting these characteristics the constitutional virtues, and I believe that the need for them is implicit in our constitutional practices. Without them, constitutional law as this society has traditionally understood it and our language today still implies is impossible. Where decision makers, and not only judges but political officials as well, exercise the constitutional virtues, they act in good faith even in the presence of ongoing disagreement over the substance of the Constitution's commands. It is possible, of course, that a constitutional system oriented in this fashion around the individual conscience will be subverted by the human tendency to bad faith, but the American constitutional experiment is a gamble, extended in time, that despite our individual and collective fallibilities, a free and decent government can rest nowhere else.

In focusing on the judiciary, and centrally on the Supreme Court of the United States,[24] I do not mean to imply that constitutional interpretation is fraught with moral significance only when it is a court that is doing the interpreting. A subsidiary theme of this book is my claim that the distinction between adjudication and constitutional decision by political actors is less dramatic than is often assumed, though not because the cynical claim that law is just "politics" in a negative sense is true. Chapter 3, in particular, attempts to show the possibility of principled constitutional interpretation in a political setting. However, there are unique elements to the decision whether a court should disregard the force of a statute or other official action in the name of the Constitution. The moral circumstances of a judge asked to exercise the power of judicial review involve considerations of constitutional structure and of what it means to call a court's judgment a "decision according to law" that are inextricably linked with his or her moral choices.

The argument of *Constitutional Conscience* proceeds in five steps. In the first chapter I discuss what I believe to be the most salient features of the moral circumstances in which a Supreme Court justice finds him- or herself when called upon to make a constitutional decision. By its structural location in the political and legal order, and by long tradition, the Court's decisions cannot be reversed except by its own action or by the cumbersome and indeed almost unworkable processes required under Article V to amend the Constitution. A five-justice majority on the nine-member Court thus enjoys the power to decide constitutional issues that is essentially unreviewable except through the noncompulsory force of public and professional criticism. For some justices, this might seem an opportunity to do good, for themselves personally or for the causes in which they believe; for others it might appear to be a temptation to misuse vast power for purposes alien to the reasons the Court is vested with such power. At the same time, a justice confronting a constitutional question will invariably justify whatever answer he or she gives in the language of the tradition. However the justice is to respond to the presence of decision-making power, if the response is inconsistent with that language, the justice is not acting in good faith.

Chapter 2 explores a common approach to addressing the issues raised by the preceding discussion. The problem confronting a justice who wishes to act in good faith is often thought to be one of how to stick to law and avoid politics in making constitutional decisions. Most proposed solutions take one of two forms. Many constitutional scholars suggest that there is a correct theory of judicial review that if followed will lead to proper, good-faith decision making. The problem with the theorists' approach, I argue, is that there is no prospect that any theory will ever attain general or even widespread assent, and that the Constitution isn't easily seen as the instantiation of a theory anyway. The other approach, which is often identified with certain well-known judges, rests the justice's obligation in the duty of good craftsmanship: a lawyerly constitutional opinion is a good constitutional opinion. There is a significant truth in this position, I agree, but it does not resolve the problem, because much of the time it is possible to write a lawyerly, well-crafted opinion coming out on either side of a seriously disputed constitutional question. In such circumstances, craftsmanship fails to instruct the justice which opinion to write, but she must still decide.

In the third chapter, I consider how a constitutional decision maker might go about making interpretive choices in addressing a constitutional question that is open to more than one plausible answer. The chapter focuses on a legal opinion that a nineteenth-century attorney general, Amos Akerman, gave the president. The issue, the opinion, and even the attorney general are long forgotten, but that is an advantage, because it eliminates the chance that either author or reader will be so committed (or opposed) to Akerman's conclusion that we will be unable to see how he got there. My purpose is to show that Akerman modeled an approach to addressing disputable questions of constitutional law that employs legal craftsmanship not to conceal difficulties or hidden springs of decision but to render them transparent and thus to enable the reader to evaluate critically the conclusions reached by the writer. Such an approach brings the language of constitutional interpretation into accord with the reality of constitutional decision, and in doing so satisfies the duties of the constitutional conscience. Chapter 3 also addresses the parallel between constitutional interpreters in the political branches (Akerman, for example) and judges making constitutional decisions. While there are differences, I conclude, they are more a matter of degree than of kind, and extreme skepticism about political-branch interpretation is unnecessary and inappropriate, and likely to be self-fulfilling.

The fourth chapter builds on the preceding one by expanding on the earlier argument by example. Not all interpreters are Akermans, so what as a general matter are the characteristics of good conscience in constitutional decision making? My answer, as the reader already knows, lies in the constitutional virtues. The relationship between these virtues and good faith in constitutional argument, I show, is not fortuitous. The Constitution, and the practices of interpretation that we have evolved to render it truly authoritative, presuppose the constitutional virtues, which are therefore an intrinsic part of the overall system, as necessary and inescapable as judicial review itself.

I address the issue of continuity in chapter 5. If we are honest about our practices, we must acknowledge that they permit and indeed require constitutional interpreters to discard old law and create new from time to time, while at the same time insisting that this process remain a process of interpretation. What (if anything), on the account I give of constitutional decision, enables us to speak of constitutional law as anything other than a series of decision points with no necessary connection over time? The answer must lie in large measure in the ongoing cultivation of the constitutional virtues, and that is possible, I suggest, primarily through the process of public discussion and criticism of the constitutional decisions of officials. Beyond that, I ask whether there is anything that one can say about the sorts of substantive decisions a virtuous interpreter ought to make? While even in principle I do not think it is possible to link the moral structure of conscientious decision too closely to an extensive set of constitutional outcomes, the constitutional virtues comport more easily with certain general lines of decision. The relationship between *how* the interpreter ought to come to a decision and *what* decision she ought to reach, however, is an evolving matter that at any given time will include areas of severe contest.

The conclusion raises what I believe to be the most fundamental question about American constitutionalism: put bluntly, is it a good idea? Our constitutional system, and this book, allow a centrality that amounts to a practical primacy to the decisions of the Supreme Court. Doing so holds together—in what might well seem a strange combination—an openness (or should we say vulnerability?) to political and ideological influence with a tendency to displace the choices of politically responsible officials with those of a small body of appointed, life-tenured justices. How is this reconcilable with our claim that the Constitution is a means of governing ourselves, not of rule by a judicial oligarchy? There is no simple answer to these questions. American constitutional law has permitted great evil at times— one need only think of slavery. And our constitutional law does privilege, for some purposes, the decisions of a professional elite headed by the Court. Our Constitution, and the practices that give it life, offer no guarantees: they are an experiment, one that rests political community on a law and a politics that must be informed by the consciences of those who make up, and speak for, that community.

There is, of course, no right or wrong answer to the question of whether this makes any sense. If it does, that sense lies in large measure in the very characteristic that may evoke anxiety, the system's resistance to closure and its correlative amenability to change.

1 ↝ The Rule of Five

Let us begin with a story about the late Justice William J. Brennan. According to his law clerks,

> [a]t some point early in their clerkships, Brennan asked his clerks to name the most important rule in constitutional law. Typically they fumbled, offering *Marbury v. Madison* or *Brown v. Board of Education* as their answers. Brennan would reject each answer, in the end providing his own by holding up his hand with the fingers wide apart. This, he would say, is the most important rule in constitutional law. Some clerks understood Brennan to mean that it takes five votes to do anything, others that with five votes you could do anything.[1]

Another version of the tale resolves the ambiguity in Brennan's explanation: "Five votes can do anything around here."[2] Hence what is now sometimes called "Justice Brennan's famed 'rule of five.'"[3]

My immediate interest in this story lies not so much in which meaning Justice Brennan intended as in the meaning that some of his clerks attributed to him, which I shall call the "strong" version of the Rule of Five: with five votes you can do anything "around here." The context of the remark was, of course, the Supreme Court as a decision-making body, even if Brennan put his question—interestingly—in terms of the most important rule in constitutional law, not in terms of the Court's institutional power. A five-justice majority on the Court, the strong Rule of Five asserts, can do anything, at least in deciding constitutional-law cases: in such cases, the conventions of American political life do not recognize any formal power to overrule a decision short of the adoption of a constitutional amendment. (The amendment process is as a practical matter little enough of a constraint on the Court. There have been four instances to date of the amendment process's being used successfully to overturn a decision of the Court . . . in over two centuries.) Furthermore, the scope of constitutional law's domain also lies by convention with the Court, so that as a practical matter the Court decides when its decisions shall be irreversible. The Court, in short, is effectively omnipotent, and, since the Court reaches substantive decisions by majority vote, the strong Rule of Five asserts that five justices can in fact exercise this omnipotent power when they choose. The strong Rule of Five thus makes a claim that, if true, lays bare a striking peculiarity about the Supreme Court's place in the American political system: the absence of effective constraints on its actions when it speaks in the name of the Constitution. The rule is also, if true, a central feature in the moral circumstances in which the justices act when they exercise as a body the power of judicial review.

But is the factual basis of the strong Rule of Five true? Don't the Court and its members face significant limitations on its, and their, freedom of action? Is it really imaginable, for example, that five justices would vote that equal protection requires government to ensure an equal distribution of property or, a bit closer to the bone for some people, that the due process clauses require the strict prohibition of all abortions because the fetus is a person within the meaning of the clauses? Many thoughtful people believe that socialism is the only morally adequate method of achieving genuine civil equality or that a fetus is an unborn child morally entitled to the same treatment given other persons. Nevertheless, there is as a practical matter no chance that the Court will adopt either view. With five votes a justice can neither ordain the classless society nor make the thoroughgoing pro-life position the supreme law of the land, no matter how eager she is to do so.

We can tease out part of the reason for these limitations on the justices' discretion by thinking a bit more about my second example of a constitutional-decision impossibility. I suspect that such a decision, holding that a fetus is legally a person, does not seem extravagant to some members of that significant group of Americans who believe that the fetus is a person morally, and yet I think few if any careful observers of the Court think the decision even a remote likelihood. This is not, as I indicated in the preceding paragraph, because the pro-life moral position is irrational or indefensible on moral grounds. The pro-life judicial decision is impossible because, in the first instance, it is beyond the realm of constitutional-law outcomes that seem plausible to the lawyers, politicians, academics, journalists, and others who make up the elite that concerns itself with constitutional law in any sustained way and from among which the justices are themselves chosen. In this context, it is a striking and significant fact, and one sometimes overlooked in the press, that the three decades since *Roe v. Wade* have seen no justice ever endorse the thorough-going pro-life position, that the fetus is a person, as a matter of constitutional law. The justices hostile to *Roe* are, jurisprudentially, not pro-life but pro-(state-)choice—as a matter of constitutional law they wish to leave the question of abortion regulation and prohibition up to the states, or at least largely so.[4]

Which moral viewpoints enjoy significant support in American society change, and so do the judgments of plausibility the constitutional elite shares about logically possible decisions by the Court. (And of course on the margin reasonable people may disagree about such matters in specific cases.) If socialism became a widely shared political conviction in American society, it is entirely likely that an equal-distribution-of-property Court decision would move from the fantastic to the conceivable. At any given time, however, the "anything" a justice with five votes can do will be bounded by what she finds it imaginable to do constitutionally, as well as, in a related way, what she finds morally imaginable as a member of that wider society in which the constitutional elite is embedded and from which, after all, it is not hermetically insulated. The moral circumstances in which justices decide constitutional-law cases include their social location within an elite subset of American society as well as, more diffusely, their membership in the society as a whole. But this reality does not constitute the sort of limitation on the Court's decisions that would invalidate the strong Rule of Five. It is more like part of the definition of the "anything" the rule decrees possible for five votes on the Court. Let us put the matter of social location to one side, therefore, and continue with another criticism of the rule, that it ignores the institutional limitations on the Court.

The Court reaches its decisions in a political environment rendering it dependent in various ways on Congress, the federal executive, state and other federal judges, and the political branches of the states in order for its orders to be more than a dead letter. Ultimately, if the constitutional law the justices announce is to shape the world effectively, the Court must have public support or at least public acquiescence. The agonizingly slow progress of Southern school desegregation in the years following *Brown v. Board of Education* demonstrates this practical boundary on the Court's ability to do "anything" in the teeth of resistance, while the now largely forgotten attacks on the Court (the Southern Manifesto, "Impeach Earl Warren!") show the possibility of a backlash aimed not just at the Court's decisions but at the Court itself. Isn't it reasonable to suppose that the justices take such limitations into account in deciding what five votes can do?

No doubt. A nineteenth-century humorist famously wrote that "th' supreme coort follows th'iliction returns,"[5] and we now know from archival research that in deciding *Brown* and other desegregation cases the justices were acutely aware of the institutional and public-opinion context of their actions.[6] Nonetheless, I think we may properly dismiss this criticism of the Rule of Five as well. The historical and social-science data suggests that public support for the Court is remarkably resilient.[7] The desegregation crisis may be something of an exception in that opposition to the Court's ruling was strong and, for a time, effective in many places, but much of the public has seemed able over time to distinguish sharp disapproval of individual decisions from disappointment in or hostility to the Court itself. Earl Warren wasn't impeached, and in recent decades, politically serious critics of the Court have focused on getting the "right" justices appointed (or the "wrong" appointments prevented) rather than on attacking the Court as an institution. Controversial decisions may face practical opposition of varying degrees of effectiveness, but there is little to suggest that the institutional limitations on the Court are of major significance in determining which constitutional positions the Court takes within the range of current plausibility (as we discussed above).[8]

So, the strong Rule of Five rests on a sound factual basis. What are the justices, and the rest of us, to make of this? What might it tell us about constitutional law, and the moral circumstances in which the justices make constitutional decisions? To assist in this inquiry, meet four members of the Court, Justices John, Johanna, Oliver, and Marsha. (Needless to say, these jurists are not only prominent but entirely fictional. Their names are borrowed, more or less, from those of the first four chief justices.)[9] All four believe that the strong Rule of Five rests on fact, and also that the rule has a significant role to play in their actions when the Court considers a constitutional case.

Justice John is financially corrupt. His vote is for sale, one way or the other, through bribes or other sorts of covert influence. He sees judging as a means of feathering his nest. In constitutional cases, nothing that might be thought to be constitutional law matters to John in determining which outcome to work for: outcomes are for the highest bidder to determine. Constitutional assertions, reasoning and logic are tools for accomplishing the goal of delivering the Court's decision in a given case, nothing more. (Considerations of plausibility are a different matter, since John's influence on his colleagues would be impaired, and the value of his vote diminished, if he advanced arguments that no one took seriously or if he lobbied for unimaginable outcomes.)[10] The strong Rule of Five is important to John because it sets the conditions of his business in vote selling, but it says nothing about constitutional law beyond showing the naïveté of a political system that gives people like John such power.

Justice Johanna would be shocked at a bribe. Her vote is the servant of her political ideals. She sees judging as a means of advancing whatever policy outcome she thinks best, based on those ideals. Her ideals do not include finding the "right" answers to legal questions, however, which is a notion she thinks intellectually bankrupt. Constitutional-law reasoning, principles, and so on, play no role, therefore, in determining what *outcome* she will work for in a constitutional case: she read between the lines in Constitutional Law I in law school and realized that constitutional law is just the decoration with which one must adorn a judicial opinion in certain sorts of cases, to appease those not in the know or unwilling to admit the truth who might otherwise be angered by a naked exertion of political power by the Court. Like John, Johanna does not want to impair her ability to get to the outcomes she wants, and so she takes more or less seriously her opinion's decorations. The strong Rule of Five states an essential feature of the American political system for her: on a broad range of policy issues, the Court makes the ultimate choice, the range of such judicial policy making being defined most of the time by the Court itself. This is, however, a truth about politics simpliciter, not about "law." Beyond decoration, there is no constitutional law to worry about.[11]

In some obvious respects, Justices John and Johanna are very unalike. John's behavior in constitutional cases, while shocking, is merely a garden-variety form of personal and professional corruption, indefensible from any perspective. He represents a problem in the enforcement of judicial ethics and criminal prohibitions, nothing more (indeed, let us trust that he will be caught, and quickly!): John himself would not say otherwise privately and understands that he is behaving in a fashion that involves deceiving his colleagues as well as the profession and the public at large. Johanna, on the other hand, truly believes that she is acting in accord with the highest standards of ethical conduct, since constitutional-law talk is only the facade courts are obliged to employ when they make policy decisions of certain sorts. She (conceivably) thinks that anyone as sophisticated as she realizes this, and that the whole elaborate apparatus of text, precedents, levels of scrutiny, briefs, and opinions is understood thus by her colleagues and other elite lawyers, and that she is not actually deceiving *them* when she circulates a memorandum or draft opinion that decorates her belief that X is better policy with sentences and paragraphs ostensibly asserting that X is required by the Constitution. To the extent that the general public believes otherwise about her (or anyone else's) published opinions, this misunderstanding no doubt serves the high public goals of social harmony and the maintenance of an orderly system of policy formulation and implementation. She would doubtless be sincerely and deeply offended if she were compared to John.

The comparison is, nevertheless, entirely appropriate. Justices John and Johanna are equally uninterested in constitutional law as a basis for decision, albeit for different reasons. For both of them the strong Rule of Five is a vital element in their activities, but its role can be no more than a pragmatic or even cynical observation about the way the Supreme Court functions. It is certainly not a "rule of constitutional law," as Justice Brennan put it. Constitutional law has nothing to do with whatever the "anything" John or Johanna wishes to accomplish except to serve as a form of ruse, even if Johanna prefers to think in terms of a Platonic noble lie. Like John, Johanna is engaged in a kind of cheating even if she believes the cheating justified by other sorts of reason. (John doesn't justify his actions, he just counts the hundred-dollar bills.) A practical proof of this harsh judgment can be found in the need Johanna would feel to avoid being found out: public disclosure of her views would bring down censure and destroy her credibility as a member of the Court, and thus her ability to advance her policy preferences. Like John, she is engaged in exercising power in ways that would not withstand scrutiny, and she knows it. No matter how lofty she thinks her ideals, she has to engage in deception to pursue them.[12]

Justice Oliver is a conscientious believer in constitutional law as the apolitical application of rules derived from the instrument's words, as well as structure, precedent, and so on. We need not worry about what range of legitimate, apolitical considerations Oliver accepts; what matters for present purposes is that his intention is to base his constitutional decisions on a fairminded interpretation of the considerations that are relevant and legitimate as a matter of law. Constitutional judging, Oliver thinks, is a matter of trying to get the Constitution's meaning and application right: that is what it means to judge a constitutional case both as a matter of internal definition and because acting in this manner is what society expects the justices to do. Oliver is fully aware of the legal realist argument that the formal arguments of the law are often inconclusive and are not the true grounds of decision and is aware of the problems with pressing the idea of a single right answer in difficult constitutional cases,[13] but he rejects the posture (he hardly thinks it an argument) that maintains that any opinion is as good as any other: from his experience as a lawyer and judge, Oliver is quite sure that there is a difference between stronger and weaker arguments, and that in the end there is a way to come to a decision between two strong arguments, and to do so without stepping outside the domain of legal reasoning.

The strong Rule of Five is important to Oliver because of the danger it represents. The Court's constitutional decisions are potentially of great political import, and the rule renders explicit what the Court's practical omnipotence permits: five justices can step outside their proper and apolitical role and announce essentially irreversible but legally illegitimate political decisions. Oliver is a charitable soul and does not suspect that his colleagues would do this consciously, but the Rule of Five creates a problem for even the most conscientious justice. Given the enormous human significance of many (by no means all) constitutional decisions, it is difficult to resist the temptation to persuade oneself that the Constitution says what one wishes it said, rather than what it really means. The Rule of Five poses, therefore, a profound threat to the moral characters of the justices by inviting them to engage in a self-deception that licenses decisions that are in fact illegitimate. The only solution to the problem the rule creates is a stern adherence to judicial duty and a commitment to vote for only those outcomes in constitutional cases that are based on the correct meaning of the Constitution. Any other course of action would be a betrayal of Oliver's oath of office and an abuse of the trust reposed in him by the American people.

Justice Oliver sometimes finds himself asked in public question-and-answer sessions if he would really vote for a morally repugnant or politically unwise outcome because he thought the Constitution required him to do so. The follow-up to his affirmative response is invariably to ask how he can justify doing so, since that would be, by definition, to perpetrate (or permit) something he himself believes is wrong. Oliver always explains patiently that the demands of the Constitution are not coterminous with the demands of justice (equality, efficiency, or whatever other values one might personally think relevant to the case) and that at times, therefore, fidelity to the Constitution will require a constitutional decision maker to adopt a position—as a justice to cast a vote—that contradicts his views on the humanly best outcome as defined by whatever extraconstitutional metric he would otherwise think it appropriate to apply. Oliver sometimes points out that we can imagine an endless list of examples: the justice who believes capital punishment immoral but who thinks it valid under the Eighth Amendment, her colleague who thinks a federal regulatory scheme inefficient and economically harmful although clearly within the scope of the interstate commerce clause, a third who sees male-only military academies as far better for national security but a clear violation of the requirement of equal protection. The problem is an old one, Oliver notes, as is its proper resolution: in one of the Supreme Court's earliest constitutional cases, *Calder v. Bull,* decided in 1798, Justice William Paterson denounced retrospective laws as having "neither policy nor safety . . . neither accord[ing] with sound legislation, nor the fundamental principles of the social compact." But Paterson concluded that for technical reasons the Constitution's ban on "ex post facto Law[s]" applies only to criminal statutes: the Constitution and political morality, for Paterson, led to contradictory conclusions about the propriety of other retrospective laws.[14] Paterson did the right thing, Oliver thinks, and experience since 1798 shows that such conflicts between the decisions of a justice about the meaning of the Constitution and his views on extraconstitutional "good" are a necessary by-product of the justice's conscientious attempt not to cheat, not to use (or try to use) the formal power to do anything in the name of constitutional law to accomplish results that are arbitrary with respect to constitutional considerations. A justice who thought otherwise would be engaged in self-deception.

I mean Justice Oliver's views to be a recognizable but kindly caricature of what most if not all modern justices, of every ideological persuasion, say in public. There have been sharp disagreements on the Court (and still more so, if possible, among the commentators) about the proper exercise of what we might call the Rule of Five power, but no member of the Court has denied his or her obligation to use that power only in obedience to the Constitution. The Court has sometimes found itself bitterly divided, not only about the correct application of the Constitution in a specific case, but also over the very tools that can properly be used in interpreting the Constitution faithfully. This sometimes leads to accusations by dissenting justices that the decision of the majority is an act of raw power, not just an error of interpretation but a willful usurpation of political power. Such criticism amounts to charging the majority with adopting Justice Johanna's approach and deciding constitutional cases on the basis of extraconstitutional policy preferences—in short, with cheating. Even under the rough standards that govern contemporary Supreme Court practice, this ugly term is not to be found, I think, in the justices' opinions, but it accurately captures the moral outrage that the language actually used by critics on and off the Court often means to communicate. The reader with doubts is invited to contemplate the opening words from a recent dissenting opinion:

> In urging approval of a constitution that gave life-tenured judges the power to nullify laws enacted by the people's representatives, Alexander Hamilton assured the citizens of New York that there was little risk in this, since "[t]he judiciary . . . ha[s] neither FORCE nor WILL but merely judgment." But Hamilton had in mind a traditional judiciary, "bound down by strict rules and precedents which serve to define and point out their duty in every particular case that comes before them." Bound down, indeed. What a mockery today's opinion makes of Hamilton's expectation. . . . . Because I do not believe that the meaning of our Eighth Amendment, any more than the meaning of other provisions of our Constitution, should be determined by the subjective views of five Members of this Court and like-minded foreigners, I dissent.[15]

And of course the same accusation can be turned on dissenters as well. These are accusations of bad faith, not descriptions of what any of the justices purports to be doing, but they are enormously suggestive witnesses to a public or at least ostensible moral consensus on the Court that "constitutional law" is dependent on the Constitution (whatever that may mean) and that the term is not in fact shorthand for "whatever the justices think best." Oliver believes that their salience lies in a shared public understanding that the justices' constitutional job is supposed to be one of apolitical decision.

We come at last to Justice Marsha. Like Justice Oliver, she acknowledges the Constitution as the only legitimate source of the Rule of Five power she can, as a practical matter, exercise in agreement with at least four of her colleagues. Unlike Oliver, however, she does not believe in the inevitability of at least occasional conflict between a justice's views about the Constitution's meaning and her views about the humanly best outcome in a constitutional case before her. In fact, Marsha believes that the Constitution mandates that the Court reach the humanly best outcome in any situation that it governs whenever that is possible.[16] Marsha understands the difficulties of balancing the best outcome for the individuals in a case against the best outcome generally, but we can leave that very difficult issue to one side. For our purposes, the crucial point is that her goal is to find the best human outcome, however the consideration of particular versus general works out. To understand her thinking, we shall have to spend more time on it than on that of her colleagues, and in the next bit I shall be retracing her reasoning rather than expressing my own unless expressly noted otherwise.

Why should a justice with five votes ever decline to reach the result she thought good in some substantive sense—as a matter of justice, equality, economic efficiency, and so on? Constitutional-law cases often involve matters that are undeniably of great human significance, and they can benefit or injure the interests and even the physical well-being of a great many people. Most of us think that a deliberate decision to impose harm on others demands some justification if it is not to be the object of moral condemnation. On the face of it, therefore, one might well think that a justice ought to have a very powerful reason not to use his power under the Rule of Five to ensure, if possible, the humanly best outcome in any constitutional case. Furthermore, as a general matter of political as well as personal ethics, one might expect a liberal and democratic society, dedicated to the proposition that governments are instituted among men to secure individual rights and promote the pursuit of happiness, to adopt a constitution designed to produce such outcomes.

Justice Oliver, of course, claims that the Court's duty to obey the Constitution overrides other responsibilities the justices might feel as individuals, but Justice Marsha thinks that is a false dichotomy, one inconsistent with the Constitution itself. Think about its opening words. The Preamble states the purposes of the instrument, or rather of the decision to make the instrument law, in terms most of which seem oriented toward human good broadly conceived rather than toward institutional goals narrowly defined. Perhaps the "more perfect Union" and the common defence are best thought of institutionally, but objectives such as establishing justice, insuring domestic tranquility, promoting the general welfare, and securing liberty to one's posterity do not seem limited as a matter of their ordinary meaning to "justice . . . unless there is a legalistic argument requiring injustice," or "tranquility . . . unless no constitutional provision permits it" and so on. It is old learning (familiar to the American founders, by the way) that a preamble to a legal instrument is not itself part of the legally operative set of commands and prohibitions established by the document, but that same learning sees a preamble as having interpretive significance by providing the point of the instrument, the reason its makers gave it legal force. If we take the Preamble in that manner, then we should interpret the legally operative institutional rules of the Constitution so as to achieve what the Preamble says is the very point of the rules— substantive justice, welfare for all, true liberty. The Constitution, the Preamble suggests, points its interpreters outside itself to a concern for worthy human purposes that the Constitution itself neither creates nor defines.

The Preamble's clear intimation that the Constitution cannot be properly read without attention to human values to be found outside the text itself is supported by many of the instrument's operative provisions and by the experience of history. The point is familiar and sometimes hotly contested with respect to some of the provisions protecting individual rights—the Constitution requires *just* compensation for the taking of property and prohibits *cruel and unusual* punishments—but can be seen elsewhere as well: the provision according Congress the power to raise money and pay debts repeats the Preamble's purposive language about the "general Welfare of the United States." At least as significantly, from the beginning of the Republic it has been clear that even questions about the proper interpretation of the Constitution's institutional arrangements may be unanswerable unless the interpreter looks to reasons that take the form of saying "This is the best [most just, equal, efficient, sensible] outcome," and for that reason the Constitution requires it. Perhaps the earliest example can be found in a question President Washington posed his secretary of state, Thomas Jefferson, in 1790: can the Senate use its power to confirm diplomatic appointments to determine the level of diplomatic office the nominee receives despite the president's designation of a specific office in the nomination? Merely to read the question is to realize that it involves a highly technical point about the proper construal of the appointments clause of Article II, Section 2, but Secretary Jefferson found it impossible to address without considering what answer would be most efficient, and he was right to think so, Marsha believes.[17] The point is not merely that textual arguments sometimes are inconclusive and require supplementation by other strictly legal forms of argument (assertions about original meaning, for example), but that even controversies about quite specific institutional details may be irresolvable unless the humanly best outcome is considered.

Justice Marsha believes that the social expectations that Justice Oliver thinks demand his understanding of the Court's role in fact support her best-outcome approach to constitutional adjudication. She finds it significant that the social-science data support her own, more impressionistic sense that most Americans are interested in the Supreme Court's decisions only for their substantive, humanly significant outcomes—not for the cogency of the justices' constitutional reasoning or the jurisprudential impact of the decisions.[18] Lawyers worry (well, some of them do) about such matters but nonlawyers are interested in the bottom line and report high levels of trust in the Court despite the almost constant announcements by disgruntled justices and op-ed writers that the majority is cheating. It is only when a decision comes to an outcome that seems humanly bizarre or repugnant to many citizens that public opinion is troubled. *Roe v.*

Wade and *Texas v. Johnson* (affording constitutional protection to abortion and flag burning, respectively) are controversial because many people are troubled by or hostile to the activities at issue; it would be silly to think that the merits or faults of the justices' reasoning in those cases had much of anything to do with the controversies over the Court's decisions. Judge Robert Bork ran into this reality in a personally unpleasant manner during the Senate Judiciary Committee hearings on his doomed nomination to the high Court. In vain Bork tried to explain that his concerns about *Griswold v. Connecticut* (protecting the use of contraceptives by married couples) were jurisprudential, rooted in his belief that the majority opinion was unprincipled and unpersuasive, rather than the product of any unwillingness to provide constitutional protection to the use of contraceptives if a sound constitutional argument could be made. Many, perhaps most, constitutional lawyers (including his many academic critics) agreed entirely with him about the *Griswold* opinion, but to the extent that Bork's stance toward *Griswold* mattered at all to public opinion, all that mattered was his perceived unwillingness to reach the publicly popular outcome.[19] There is, in fact, every reason to think that most Americans want the Supreme Court to come to the humanly best outcome in constitutional cases. It would be bizarre to think that the Court should insist on refusing to interpret the Constitution to achieve such outcomes if the people clearly want them to do so. After all, it is ultimately the people's Constitution, not the lawyers', as none other than James Madison wrote long ago.[20]

Justice Oliver would doubtless respond that the very point of the Constitution is to put limits on what public opinion can accomplish. Justice Marsha agrees that is true, but true only in a different sense from the one Oliver intends. A constitutional limitation such as the First Amendment does indeed function as a limit on the ability of a transitory majority to translate its views into law, but the best-outcome approach is supported by the ongoing stance of a continuing majority. Furthermore, Oliver is himself a de facto adherent of Marsha's approach, although Marsha graciously concedes that he is so unwittingly. The proof lies in the observable behavior of the Court and its members. Whatever their language, in constitutional cases modern justices appear to vote for what they regard as the best outcome. Political-science studies of the justices' behavior differ over the relative weight to give simple policy preferences and institutional concerns in explaining the justices' choices but almost always give short shrift to "law" as a constraining force on the Court's outcomes.[21] (In case you are wondering, there appears to be no difference in political-science terms between "liberal" and "conservative" justices in this regard.) What that means, the political scientists often imply, is that all justices are like Justice Johanna, deciding cases on extra-constitutional bases while cloaking their reasons in constitutional decorations. Marsha strongly disagrees. This description of the Court's practices rests on an implicit assumption that decisions driven by the justices' views on the humanly best outcome are by that token not driven or constrained by "law." But that dichotomy, which the political scientists share with Oliver, is precisely what Marsha rejects as unfounded in the constitutional text and unnecessary to the practice of faithful judging. What the political-science data show in fact is that the dichotomy is incoherent, an insistence that what the Supreme Court regularly does when it decides constitutional cases is something other than constitutional law.

That makes no sense. The Supreme Court is, without any dispute, the most important actor in the formal articulation of constitutional law. It is odd indeed—indeed, virtually incoherent—to think that the most important participant in some activity is not in fact engaged in that activity, but rather doing something else altogether. Yet that is what the usual policy/law dichotomy unavoidably implies. Justice Marsha believes that her approach, in contrast, is simple and persuasive common sense: the Court's activities define what "doing constitutional law" is. This by no means precludes criticisms of the Court's decisions, but it identifies what sensible criticism ought to rest on: arguments that the majority failed to reach the outcome that was *in fact* the humanly best outcome possible in terms of justice (equality, efficiency, etc.)—in other words, that the majority did the job it meant to do poorly or unsuccessfully, not the familiar jeremiad, now revealed to be specious, that the majority justices were cheating because they weren't even trying to do constitutional law. Justices who decide constitutional cases on the basis of their view of the best outcome in terms of justice (or whatever) are in no way cheating or usurping a role not theirs.

Justice Marsha thinks the cumulative effect of the last several observations is overwhelming: what she is doing is what American society appears to want and expect, and it is in fact the practice of the major institutional actor in constitutional debate. In short, she is doing exactly what a sensible person would think her oath demands: she is observing both the social expectations that accompany her office as a justice and the definition of constitutional decision making implicit in the actual practice of constitutional law. She finds it difficult to see what more could be asked of her.

Justice Marsha is aware that critics sometimes scorn her understanding of constitutional law as a naive search for a chimerical "perfect Constitution" that ignores the imperfect historical reality of the actual Constitution.[22] This criticism is, she thinks, unfounded. She fully acknowledges that the Court's Rule of Five power, and her own participation in that power, stem entirely from the Constitution, and she is confident that her belief that this power ought to be used to reach the humanly best outcomes in constitutional cases rests firmly on the outward-pointing language of the Constitution itself, not solely on her views about how it makes sense for a liberal and democratic society to set up its constitutional arrangements. (She does think that the humanly-best-outcome understanding of constitutional law makes good sense, but that is a backward-looking consideration that supports her reading of the Constitution's language: it is the language that provides the foundation for her view.) Of course she acknowledges that the Constitution's operative language needs to be treated seriously—it is the operative provisions, after all, that give rise to constitutional cases and to the Court's power of decision in the first place. Much of the Constitution's language and many of the institutions it creates or presupposes are historically conditioned: think of direct taxes, the writ of habeas corpus, and indictments by grand jury. Many of its provisions, furthermore, are arbitrary in relationship to human good, however defined, in much the same way as a law ordaining on which side of the road cars shall drive is neutral. The question must be settled, but it hardly matters which way. (Indeed, some constitutional provisions address matters that could have been ignored altogether.)

Justice Marsha admits and indeed insists that whatever constitutional language is relevant to the case at hand must be treated seriously, and she concedes that as a result the justices have to deal on occasion with provisions that simply may not be susceptible to best-outcome analysis without an intolerable abuse of the provisions' wording.[23] There is no way to keep a straight face while arguing for a judicial decision that Article I, Section three ("The Senate . . . shall be composed of two Senators from each State"), must be read to require that Senate seats be distributed proportionately to each state's population in order to satisfy the Constitution's requirement of equal protection, especially when the inconvenient fact of Article V's language ("no State, without its Consent, shall be deprived of its equal Suffrage in the Senate") comes to mind.[24] As a consequence, it would be wrong to hold unconstitutional the states' equality in the Senate even on the basis of a well-founded belief that justice and equality require proportional representation. But she thinks this both a small and ultimately an illusory embarrassment for her best-outcomes approach: small because very few constitutional provisions as difficult to subject to a best-outcome reading as this one play any role whatever in actual constitutional disputes, and illusory because the humanly best outcome in a case like the senatorial-equality hypothetical is to respect the constitutional language.[25] The lesson of history is that the great majority of constitutional disputes arise out of provisions that are facially susceptible as a matter of wording to best-outcome readings (commerce, free speech, due process) or involve issues under a linguistically particular clause that are not determined by the clause's specific language.[26]

For Justice Marsha, the strong Rule of Five is neither an opportunity to cheat, financially or intellectually, nor a temptation to judicial overreaching. It is, rather, a logical feature of the institutional arrangements the Constitution ordains. Having as its goal justice, welfare, equal protection, and so on, the Constitution has established a system, constitutional decision making by the Supreme Court, by which controversies about how well other parts of government have met these constitutional goals may be measured and, where necessary, corrected. Marsha thinks of herself as a profound constitutional conservative, and would do so regardless of what ideological label the evening news gives her. Marsha does not see her position as equivalent to the proposition that "the Constitution is what the judges say it is" in the sense that the Court just picks and chooses what a majority of its members prefer: her position is that the Constitution is what the justices *rightly* say it is.[27]

Justice Marsha (who now retires to her chambers, with our thanks) has put sharp questions to the viewpoint that Justice Oliver is meant to represent, Oliver's being the one that (as the reader will recall) all recent nominees to the Court have shared. What is at stake in the strong version of Justice Brennan's Rule of Five (with five votes you can do anything) is now clearer. The standard distinction Oliver draws between making decisions (legitimately) according to the Constitution and making decisions (illegitimately) on extraconstitutional bases turns out to be neither as clear as is usually assumed nor indeed the Court's actual practice, and not even possible, at least if the distinction is understood along the lines of the usual rhetoric. It is unclear because Marsha has as good a claim to be acting in accord with this society's expectations for the Supreme Court as Oliver. Oliver's distinction is contrary to the Court's actual practice: as Marsha points out, the justices appear to act fairly consistently in accordance with we can pejoratively call their policy preferences or more benignly term their views on the humanly best outcomes in constitutional cases. Oliver's distinction is, furthermore, impossible to observe in practice: not only does some of the Constitution's language appear to invite attention to extraconstitutional values, but the instrument also generates at least some (many, I think) constitutional questions, including questions of a technical nature as well as the grand, headline-stealing issues, to which an answer cannot be determined without resort to resources beyond text, structure, and history. Oliver's mainstream viewpoint, in short, is not the position to which a conscientious justice must inexorably come. Indeed, for those who share Marsha's perspective, Oliver's is not in fact a position to which a truly self-aware justice can honestly adhere. The logical corollary of Marsha's position is that Oliver is engaged in self-deception. Or worse.

As Patrick Brennan has nicely put it in a related context, "the bell announcing Legal Realism cannot be unrung":[28] no modern lawyer can believe in good faith that law can be nothing more than the logical working-out of rules that do not require the exercise of contestable judgment for their interpretation and application. If Justice Marsha's arguments about the actual practice of constitutional law make sense, it is unacceptable simply to repeat as bromides, noble lies, or judicially self-protective decoration Justice Oliver's apolitical description of what the Court does or should do. That description is, in substantial measure, false and deceptive. As such, it is destructive to the political community of the American Republic, which, like all political communities, depends on good-faith behavior on the part of those who act on its behalf (whether judges, political officials, voters, or citizen-critics). It will not do, in the long run, for justices to pretend to be doing one thing while they are in fact doing something quite different; it is not acceptable, in the immediate here and now, for them to pretend at all. If our practices of constitutional law require of the practitioners morally objectionable actions, then our practices need to be discarded lest we be ruled by those willing to sacrifice their consciences to their political interests. Yes, of course one's political interests are a matter of conscience (unless one is Justice John), but their pursuit through deceptive means is wrong both for those who see the wrongness entirely in terms of the impact on the community and for those who see good faith as a moral obligation quite apart from its disutility. Marsha's truths render Oliver's claims indefensible.

Unfortunately, we cannot simply substitute Justice Marsha's position for Justice Oliver's: she too is caught in an internal contradiction that invalidates her view as surely as Oliver's. Her approach to constitutional decision making, the reader will recall, is to seek what is truly the best human outcome in the controversy presented to the Court, not just to decree her own individual preference. The problem, of course, is that decisions about the best human outcome depend, much of the time, on substantive and highly contestable accounts about what is, in fact, the human good. The American political community is deeply divided, on principle, over such accounts, like all modern, large societies.[29] In no realistically imaginable universe will we agree in detail, and even on many broad issues, about what is good and evil for individuals and groups of our species.[30] One of the moral circumstances in which justices decide constitutional cases is the existence of this sort of profound ethical discord. A self-honest justice has to understand that when she announces a decision resting on a contestable moral judgment she speaks not for the community of the Republic but for those within that community who agree with her, and that her decision will be opposed by others who hold with equal conviction opposite views. Recognizing this fact entails no surrender to moral relativism. Marsha's may be the moral truth and she may be certain—rightly—that it is. But within the public discourse of the Republic there is no moral high ground from which she can prove her case on ethical grounds. And in the absence of that moral high ground her perspective on the strong Rule of Five collapses.

At least in cases not driven by obstinately precise constitutional text, the Court does not replace mistaken views of the Constitution's goals with correct ones: it merely substitutes the debatable views of a majority of, say, Congress with the equally debatable views of five or more justices. As a matter of political theory, this seems impossible to defend on any democratic premises. In the terms of this book, it requires Justice Marsha to defend her honesty in announcing her decisions as constitutional by insisting that those who conscientiously disagree with those decisions are simply wrong. As a judgment by an individual, I think that insistence entirely proper (even if humility may lead us to be slow to come to it in individual instances): if you and I disagree on, say, theological grounds about the morality of abortion, one of us may very well be right in God's eyes and the other wrong. The same claim, made as a judgment by someone acting on behalf of the political community, announcing the content of a norm of that community, is quite different. If I as an individual pronounce your view on abortion wrong, I differentiate us as individuals and (perhaps) along religious or other lines that distinguish groups within our society. If I as the authorized and official speaker of the Republic's norms pronounce your view on abortion wrong, I define you as, on that issue at any rate, outside the community of the Republic. That such judgments can and sometimes must be made can be taken for granted (think of the conscientious would-be slaveowner). That such judgments can be a regular feature of constitutional adjudication by the Court is a view that threatens to transform judicial review into a means of partisan dispute. If that is the end to which Marsha's perspective leads, I and many others will find it unacceptable. To borrow something the great Learned Hand wrote, I would find it most irksome to be ruled by a bevy of Platonic Guardians, and even if I were willing to be, I wouldn't choose the justices for the job. There must be a better view of their role, and an obvious place to look for it is in the expectations the justices themselves accept as defining their job. In this chapter we have used those expectations critically, as a means of identifying the moral problems that beset the positions held by our four justices. In the next, we shall explore what constructive use one can make of the same expectations.

2 ⤺ Playing the Game

Learned Hand is that rare example of a judge who lingers in American memory—American professional memory, to be sure—although he was never a member of the Supreme Court of the United States. Hand is the source, furthermore, of an anecdote central to the memory of a judge who did serve on the Court, Oliver Wendell Holmes, Jr.:

> I remember once I was with [Justice Holmes]; it was a Saturday when the Court was to confer. It was before we had a motor car, and we jogged along in an old coupe. When we got down to the Capitol, I wanted to provoke a response, so as he walked off, I said to him: "Well, sir, goodbye. Do justice!" He turned quite sharply and he said: "Come here. Come here." I answered: "Oh, I know, I know." He replied: "That is not my job. My job is to play the game according to the rules."[1]

Holmes is famous (or infamous) for arguing that one can best understand the law by purging one's thought of moral considerations.[2] This story, as it is often understood, shows Justice Holmes enunciating a perspective on law that divorces positive law—the law that courts enforce—from the concerns for justice and fairness that originate in so-called ethical perspectives.[3] Many people read Holmes in just this way, and understood in this manner, Hand's story seems to corroborate the accusation that Holmes was "a bitter and lifelong pessimist" for whom "the function of law . . . is simply to channel private aggressions in an orderly, perhaps in a dignified, fashion."[4] Taken as a guide to judicial conduct, this understanding of the story draws a sharp line between coming to decisions that are just because they are just and coming to decisions because they are the logical out-working of some set of authoritative norms whose authority has nothing substantive to do with justice.

Whatever the truth about Justice Holmes's views generally, Judge Hand did not understand the "do justice" incident in this way. Discussing Holmes's significance to the law, Hand wrote that Holmes "was to me the master craftsman certainly of our time; and he said: 'I hate justice,' which he didn't quite mean. What he did mean was this." Hand then recounted the story I've just quoted.[5] It isn't self-evident, to be sure, how Hand thought the anecdote explains why (or in what sense) Holmes wasn't entirely serious about hating justice. But Hand's take on an event that he and Holmes and perhaps a driver were alone in witnessing should give us pause before interpreting the story as clear support for the claim that Holmes was a legal positivist uninterested in the moral significance of his actions as a judge.

If Justice Holmes didn't intend Judge Hand (or the rest of us) to think he meant playing according the rules excludes doing justice, what might his point have been? The existence of numerous variations on the story gives us a possible clue. It is clear that the oldest version, and the one most likely to capture what Holmes actually said, is Hand's. As the reader will recall, according to Hand, Holmes said, "My job is to play the game according to the rules." In some versions, however, this becomes some form of "I just make sure that people play by the rules."[6] These are very different statements. Making sure that (other) people "play by the rules" is a description of the role of the judiciary, or perhaps of the Supreme Court in particular, that treats the justices' actions as the imposition on other people of norms that are external both to the justices and to those who must obey the Court's decrees. A justice decides what he believes is the correct disposition of the case without regard to what he personally believes about the ethical weight of the conflicting claims, just as he is undeterred by the thought that the losing party will almost certainly find nothing in the Court's decision but the imposition of impersonal rules of which the Court claims to be the oracle. The justices sit apart from the conflict of moral claims that inevitably accompanies and often inspires legal conflict: they are alienated and almost alien observers themselves both of the rules they enforce and the people on whom they enforce those rules. This does not entail the conclusion that the rules themselves are not moral in content or source. They may indeed be the Moral Order of the Universe, but the justices do not enforce them for that reason but simply because they are in the rule book that an abstraction called "the law" has provided. Whatever the external sources or justification of the rules the Court imposes, it does so because they are the rules. "I just make sure that people play by the rules" is a thoroughly authoritarian description of what the justices are about, and perhaps not coincidentally a description that is easily assimilable to the view of Holmes as a nihilistic hater of justice.[7]

In contrast, in Judge Hand's rendition of the story (which I shall henceforth treat as the original, and ascribe to Holmes), Holmes situated himself as a justice *within* a certain activity or practice: "My job is to play the game according to the rules." Holmes was not saying that he was a referee or umpire external to the game but rather that he was someone engaged in playing it himself. It is significant that Holmes made this point in language that had for him personal, moral weight. As Michael Herz has noted, "'job' was a loaded term for Holmes," one that suggested a role that was "a form of service . . . [of] 'practical altruism.'"[8] Holmes responded to Hand's perhaps-jocular exhortation to "do justice" in terms—my job, the game, playing by the rules—that were not for Holmes amoral or alienating. However strange to many (most?) of us, for Wendell Holmes this way of talking seems very unlikely to have been an attempt to remove the role of the judge from the sphere of the ethical. It was instead, I suggest, a terse and somewhat cryptic identification of where it is within the sphere of ethics one can properly locate judicial decision making. The job of the judge is freighted with moral significance, but that ethical weight should not be seen in terms of an abstract or generalized notion of justice. Judicial decision making brings with it obligations and demands moral commitments, but of a sort different (in part anyway) from those duties and commitments evoked by other situations. "My job is to play the game according to the rules": by virtue of his "job," his role as a member of the Court, Holmes was himself under obligations which defined the ethical significance of his judicial decisions and the limitations on what he could do in that role.[9] But this implies that the activity of judging cannot be separated from the point of the game the justices are playing, or the moral content of the rules they follow, or indeed the impact of their decisions on those affected by their decisions.

In describing his job as playing the game according to the rules, Justice Holmes did not attempt to define the point of "the game," the practice of judging (or more narrowly, Supreme Court decision making). Nor did he explain what in fact the rules that define the practice are. Instead, he expressed a certain attitude— a moral attitude—toward his place within that practice. Whatever it means to act as a judge, and whatever the point of society giving people that role, as a justice of the Supreme Court Holmes's job, as he saw it, was to fill the role, to play the game as (I think we may interpolate) people generally understand the game, according to the rules generally accepted. If you are playing chess (and not something else), you can't make bishops leap over pawns no matter how desirable it would be if they could; if you are judging Supreme Court cases (and not doing something else), you can't pursue a goal if doing so would take you beyond the rules that define what judging such cases is. Not because you don't care about moral obligations such as justice, but precisely because you do care. The obligation to remain within the role is itself a moral obligation.

Justice Holmes, if this is right, was not denying, but rather insisting on the presence of a moral dimension to the role of the judge. That, however, simply takes us to another question: What are the ethical duties and commitments that are particular

to the role of the judge? (Quick promissory note, to be re-
deemed in chapter 3: the fact that these duties and commitments are part of what it means to be a judge does not mean
they may not play a similar part in other roles.) Holmes's answer (as I construe his meaning) is that judging is not an exercise in simply choosing what one prefers, for whatever reason
one chooses, even if that reason rests on the highest of moral
but extralegal principles. The great legal historian Alan Watson once wrote, "The judge cannot say: 'This is my judgment
because I like it.'"[10] Watson thinks this prohibition is a defining feature of law, which suggests that Justice Johanna's view
of her job in constitutional decision making not only is contrary
to American society's general understanding of the Court's
place in the constitutional order, but would also be in the deepest sense lawless on any court. In any event, Holmes's statement
to Hand accords with the view expressed by Watson (and Justices Oliver and Marsha): Holmes thought that the justices of
the Supreme Court are supposed to play a game, an ordered,
rule-bound activity, not to pick and choose what they like, even
if what they prefer is justice in some ethical or political sense.
Where there is more than one plausible solution to a question
of constitutional law, by common understanding the authority
of the answer proposed, whether by the Court or anyone else,
ultimately must rest somewhere other than on the identity of
the answerer. Whatever else one may say about those intellectual perspectives that deny the possibility of political and legal
decision on any basis other than the preferences of the decision
maker, they are utterly destructive of anything resembling the
traditional practice of constitutional law.

The problem with Justice Holmes's dictum is that it doesn't
tell us anything specific about the game the justices are (or ought
to be) playing or the rules that bind them except that they rule
out Justice Johanna's view of her job. (From this point on, I shall
be talking about constitutional decision making by the justices
of the Supreme Court, although Holmes almost certainly was
speaking more broadly. Furthermore, for present purposes what

Holmes himself thought is not the issue.) No one can fault two young children who play with the chess board and chessmen however they wish because they are innocent of the rules of chess, but it is intrinsic to the very notion of a game that there be some rules and that those rules be known to the players, although that is also consistent with there being large areas of discretion and even means by which the rules can change. It isn't clear to me that a constitutional decision-making game in which the only rules are that a justice picks her favored outcome (on whatever basis, from the Moral Order to mere whimsy), and then must provide a document in legalese that pretends to justify that outcome, really ought to be considered a rule-bound activity at all, but in the actual context of American society that issue need not be resolved, because even if such an activity counts as a game for some purposes, as we saw in the previous chapter this is not the game that the justices purport to be playing, or that Americans generally think they are playing. As a matter of political practice, "[w]e are under a Constitution, but the Constitution is what the judges say it is," as Charles Evans Hughes said a century ago.[11] But this society's general acquiescence in judicial review rests on the assumption that political practice is normative *only* when it accords with the Constitution, and that includes the practice of judicial review by the high Court. The legitimacy of the Court's decisions depends on the perception that the justices are playing the game according to the rules.

Chief Justice Hughes came to regret the comment I quoted:

> This remark has been used, regardless of its context, as if permitting the inference that I was picturing constitutional interpretation by the courts as a matter of judicial caprice. This was farthest from my thought. . . . I was speaking of the essential function of the courts under our system in interpreting and applying constitutional safeguards.[12]

"Interpreting and applying" constitutional safeguards—not making them up. There are, it appears, more and different rules to the constitutional decision-making game than the simple positivist assertion that the Supreme Court has the last word, than the strong Rule of Five as the substance of constitutional law. If the justices (and we) are to make practical use of Holmes's dictum about the justices playing the game according to the rules, these rules must be identified.

The simplest answer is that the rules are those expressed in the words of the constitutional text. Playing the constitutional-law game involves figuring out what the words require, permit, or prohibit. That may be more difficult, of course, than interpreting a grocery list or the installation instructions for a software program (well, perhaps not the latter), but it is in principle no different an enterprise, and so the constitutional-law game becomes one that involves nothing more than an understanding of words and is, furthermore, a game with right answers. To vary our imagery, playing constitutional law is analogous to doing crossword puzzles. Justice Oliver, in at least some moods, is inclined toward this understanding of his task as a justice. Unfortunately, as we saw in the last chapter, this won't do. It isn't an honest description of what the justices actually do, and it isn't possible even in principle. The reader will recall the example I gave of President Washington's 1790 question to Secretary Jefferson, a question that clearly had to have an answer under our Constitution and, equally clearly, could not be answered by staring at the words of the text, no matter how long, how sincerely, or how intelligently. "Clause-bound interpretivism," as John Hart Ely labeled it in his great book *Democracy and Distrust*, is (as he said) simply an impossibility. Ely's argument emphasized not so much the absence of textual answers to undeniably constitutional questions as the indeterminacy of many of the more important provisions in the text: "[T]he objection to interpretivism is that it is incomplete, that there are clauses it cannot rationalize."[13] But his argument and Justice Marsha's are simply the two halves of a consistent and convincing whole. Clause-bound interpretivism is not inaccurate as a description of our actual practice of constitutional law because the justices at some point

fell away from the true, interpretivist faith—a motif sometimes entertained by scholars sympathetic to Justice Oliver.
It is inaccurate because it cannot make sense of what it purports to be interpreting. The constitutional text itself presupposes that its interpreters will go outside the four corners of
its language.

Professor Ely's attack on clause-bound interpretivism should
have carried the day, and no doubt did with many of his readers,
and his own solution to defining the rules of the constitutional-
law game shaped much of the next quarter century of constitutional scholarship. The proper role of the judiciary in exercising
the power of judicial review, Ely argued, can be defined by identifying the right theory of judicial review. Ely's own nomination
was that judicial review is legitimate (chiefly) when it addresses
problems with the system of representative democracy that is
the ordinary means by which the American Republic makes
political decisions. Where something has gone amiss with the
methods by which elected officials are chosen—for example,
through interference with free speech, gerrymandering intended
to reduce political opposition to impotence, or the effective exclusion of "discrete and insular minorities" from the political process—the Supreme Court has license and indeed responsibility to
intervene broadly on constitutional grounds.[14] Where the processes of representative democracy are functioning, the Court's
role is much narrower, although Ely conceded, as did Justice Marsha in our previous chapter, that in dealing with constitutional
provisions that have a clear meaning or application, the Court
rightly deals with words rather than theory.[15]

Unfortunately, Professor Ely's theory-based approach to defining the rules of the constitutional-law game does not resolve
our problem. Its subsequent history gives an indication why:
Ely has had many admirers but few followers. In the wake of *Democracy and Distrust* a cottage industry arose of constitutional-
law scholars who shared Ely's desire for a theory that would
escape the limitations of clause-bound interpretivism but who
found Ely's own proposal faulty.[16] The result of a lot of hard

intellectual work by many of the smartest academic lawyers in the business has been the production of almost as many theories as there are theorists, and no reason to think that any of these theories will ever command wide support among the scholars or any particular allegiance by the justices. As a practical matter, the theory enterprise, to be blunt, hasn't worked, in the sense that no one, not even Ely, has come even remotely close to persuading the politicians, judges, or lawyers—much less the American public—to adopt any particular theory. The theories all remain academic, in the most negative sense.

That is as it should be. The search for the right constitutional theory is wrong in principle because no theory can satisfy the first condition for its success, the provision of a persuasive argument that the theory really ought to be attributed to the Constitution. The Court's own practices, as we have seen, conform to no theory other than the unattractive one of ideological choice by the individual justices, and there is no other common basis on which a theory could rest. The text of the Constitution is resolutely atheoretical, at least when one goes beyond generalizations about separation of powers and the rule of law that no one would contest and that do not clearly resolve any of the constitutional questions that actually trouble us. A few of the founders, James Madison in particular, had interesting views about the relationship between the Constitution and political theory, but that gives us no reason to treat those views as implicit or unwritten provisions of the Constitution. (It is now widely and correctly understood that the canonization of the *Federalist* papers is an artifact of legal argument, and one that the Court, which did much to create it, ignores when convenient.)[17] As Justice Joseph Story wrote long ago, "Nothing but the text was adopted by the people."[18] If clause-bound interpretivism is impossible, constitutional theory in the Ely tradition is equally so, because it is groundless: it can in fact be nothing other than the imposition onto the only indisputable common ground, the Constitution, of ideas that are eminently disputable. Any and all constitutional theories are simply sets of ideological and political positions that can be rejected without any disloyalty or disobedience to the Constitution.[19] It is the text that we share as a society, and whatever approach the justices take to their job must somehow find its rules of the game in (or in relationship to) the text. Ely's sort of theory cannot do that any more than can clause-bound interpretivism.

The judiciary's lack of interest in the work of the theorists is a fact that I think deserves more attention than it gets from most scholars. An important source of this judicial attitude, I believe, is that the theorists have generally shared, as a goal, the search for a means, an intellectual technology, that can prevent judges from importing politics (or the wrong sort of politics) into constitutional law. The judges, in contrast, have always recognized (if implicitly) what the theorists are reluctant to admit, that there is no technological means of excluding politics from constitutional law: "Thus, the Court must face political questions in legal form. . . . Controversies over [the Constitution's] meaning often spring from political motives, for the object of politics always is to obtain power. . . . And all constitutional interpretations have political consequences."[20] The traditional judicial approach to achieving fidelity to the rules of the game has been moral, not technical, in character. By a set of ideas and images, American judges have endeavored to cultivate loyalty to a certain objectivity, rationality, and neutrality in law, and a distance from the passion, willfulness, and self-interest of electoral politics. And the most powerful image which they have invoked is that of the judge as the disciplined spokesperson of an apolitical, or at any rate nonpartisan, law.

Academic lawyers and political scientists sometimes speak contemptuously of "oracular" theories of judging, and indeed some expressions of the judge as the mere mouthpiece of the law cannot be taken too seriously, but the criticism is too shallow, and contempt is out of place: much of the time what is being expressed is a profoundly moral commitment to acting not from and on behalf of the judge's personal politics or faction but in service to the community, to the government of laws and not of men. This image, of the judge or court as speaking for the community, is very old. Writing in 1794, in one of the very first cases of judicial review of legislation, the great Jeffersonian jurist Spencer Roane wrote that in cases of public law judges "are bound to decide, and they do actually decide on behalf of the people."[21] Two centuries later, a federal court of appeals explained that "[j]udges speak the voice of the law. In doing so, they speak for and to the entire community."[22] Invoking this image does not make it so, of course; the implicit hope has been that incorporating it into a complex, ongoing tradition of thought and discussion might make the image part of the judge's life, shaping or reshaping the springs of decision.

To a moral commitment to act for the community as a whole and in service of its governance by law, American judges have usually added a commitment to act with a cautious mistrust of their own freedom from the subtle pressures and appeals of sheerly political preference. Consider, for example, Justice Harry Blackmun's comments in his opinion in *Furman v. Georgia*, a seminal death penalty case. Rejecting arguments about the inefficacy and barbarity of capital punishment, Blackmun wrote,

> This, for me, is good argument, and it makes some sense. But it is good argument and it makes sense only in a legislative and executive way and not as judicial expedient. [I]f I were a legislator, I would do all I could to sponsor and to vote for legislation abolishing the death penalty. . . . I do not sit on these cases, however, as a legislator. . . . We should not allow our personal preferences as to the wisdom of legislative and congressional action, or our distaste for such action, to guide our judicial decision in cases such as these. The temptations to cross that policy line are very great.[23]

Observers often dismiss this sort of language as naive or written in bad faith: the very judge who piously utters such platitudes this time will be pressing his or her "personal preferences" in the next case. Once again, however, I think that the criticism is partially correct but too shallow. Justice Blackmun and the many judges who have expressed similar sentiments are not asserting a Pollyanna-like unwillingness to acknowledge the role of personal preference and prejudice in judicial decision making, but something rather the opposite: a kind of asceticism of the mind and will that is meant to respond to and check the "temptations" of politics.

Perhaps the most flamboyant exponent of what I take to be the judges' own traditional answer to the law-and-politics problem was Felix Frankfurter. Frankfurter's opinions while a justice on the Supreme Court often discuss at length the judge's duty to subordinate his individuality as a political person in order to be able to speak for the legal tradition, but his most striking image was formulated in private correspondence: "I have an austere and even sacerdotal view of the position of a judge on this Court. . . . When a priest enters a monastery, he must leave—or ought to leave—all sorts of worldly desires behind him. And this Court has no excuse for being unless it's a monastery."[24] The picture of Supreme Court justices as political monks is so extreme and so imprecise a description of their actual behavior that it may seem a bit silly, but I believe that Frankfurter was stating in his typically overheated way a view broadly shared in the American legal tradition. When they ascend the bench, judges should put away politics of the evening-news sort, and if they do not do so, they fail to play the game according to the rules.

As I've no doubt already suggested, the rhetoric of apolitical judging, as a solution to the problem of how to play the game, captures part of what it might mean for judges to be something other than Justice Johanna. Even in overstatements like Frankfurter's monastic imagery there is a sort of high moral seriousness, a noble aspiration to subordinate self to the needs of the community. But in the end, the judges' approach is not an answer, or at least not a complete one, for several reasons. First, many observers would say that the judges' efforts to exclude politics from law by moral effort have not been notably successful over time and in any event are in an advanced stage of decay at present. A line of moral thought unable to shape decisively the moral practices to which it is directed is of dubious value to anyone.

Secondly, the judicial aspiration of abstention from politics renders incoherent or impossible the judicial task in cases in which the standard tools of legal interpretation do not provide a clear resolution—that is to say, the very cases we are worried about. Phrased as the judges often put it, the injunction to make decisions according to law and not politics is by itself empty. Viewed apart from the interpreter's broader moral and political commitments, the "law" to which the judge is instructed to adhere is indeterminate in such cases, a cipher, incapable of guiding decision.

Fundamentally, however, I am not satisfied with the judiciary's solution because it is flawed in its very conception. To explain what I mean, I must ask the reader to recall a basic premise of our system: the political order of the United States aspires to be a government of laws, not of men. In order to safeguard this aspiration, the political order has accorded public law, administered by the courts, the tasks of separating the spheres of law and politics and of confining the political with the legal. And judges have striven to enable themselves to execute these tasks by trying to renounce the political out of loyalty to the legal. At each step there is a dichotomy and a choice, and at each step after the first, the dichotomy and choice denigrate politics. Inscribed in the entire enterprise, as indeed in the parallel efforts of the constitutional theorists to specify a methodology of decision making, is a fundamental fear and dislike of the political, of the world of passion, interest, disagreement, struggle, compromise, choice.

It is a bit startling to notice that a political order rests on a devaluation of the political, but the problem goes deeper than paradox or irony. The mainstream American legal tradition's understanding of how to play the game is fundamentally Manichaean. The implicit images it ascribes to politics will be familiar ones to the theologically literate: the American legal tradition has restated in a modern and institutional context the ancient dualistic dislike of the world of change, passion, and particularity, and it has revived as well the ancient dualistic solution of sharply dividing the eternal and the temporal, the pure and the dirty, the spiritual and the earthly. Ancient Jewish and Christian opponents of dualism could have predicted the consequences. The American legal mainstream's implicit strategy for achieving the deepest moral purpose of the system of law has been to identify a spiritual elite and then to impose on that elite an insupportable and ultimately disabling demand for purity. The resulting mix of arrogance, failure, self-deceit, and loss of faith should be no surprise.

One conclusion that could be drawn at this point is that the problem of how to play the game goes all the way back to the American ambition of establishing a government of laws and not of men. If men were angels, no government would be necessary, Madison wrote.[25] But men and women are not angels, and any government they fashion will be a matter of politics, a government of men and women and not of laws. There can be no completely autonomous role for law in society, and consequently no place for loyalty to law, to the exclusion of politics. There are political, moral, and spiritual demands on our capacity for faith and commitment, but the notion of professing allegiance to "the law" in some pure form is empty or pernicious. This is a view that has many adherents in political science departments, and not a few (usually unacknowledged) within law faculties. At first glance, indeed, it seems to present a coherent understanding of the role of judges—that of Justice Johanna: judges are simply politicians, who must and should act to advance their own views of the best political outcome.

But this isn't satisfactory, either. As I argued in chapter 1, judges who understand themselves to be politicians and nothing more must make decisions that at least at times are faithless to what the political community as a whole views as their duty. This is a recipe for personal moral catastrophe. It is the conclusion that for judges to do their jobs they must decline to keep faith with their fellow citizens.

The other point I want to make, which was implicit in chapter 1 although to state it clearly requires the argument in this chapter as well, is that I do not think the judge-as-politician view can be confined to some set, small or large, of politically controversial decisions. Once accepted, I think that this position will eat up all the reasons for subordinating one's "personal" beliefs about the right outcome in any case to the outcome that ostensibly results from application of traditional legal argument. Once the aspiration of playing the game according to the rules is emptied of meaning, it is difficult for me to see why a judge should decline to follow her political inclinations whenever she can. And in short order, I suspect that judges would not feel any hesitancy in doing so, regardless of whether their inclinations rest on high moral principle or narrow partisan allegiance. If we surrender the aspiration of Holmes's idea that the job of the justice is to play the game, we will indeed give up any distinctive place for law at all.

We seem to have come to an impasse parallel to the one with which chapter 1 concludes: the Constitution as text is, at least by societal stipulation, the governing authority that ought to supply the rules of the game, but the justices (and we) cannot honestly play the game either by linguistic purism ("hand me the dictionary") or by invoking a grand theory ("hand me Ely, or whomever"), or by resolving to keep to the straight and narrow path of legal craftsmanship ("hand me the collected opinions of Justice Frankfurter"). The way out of the problem, or (better) the way into the game that Justice Holmes thought the Court ought to play according to the rules, begins with the argument that Professor Philip Bobbitt has been advancing for many years.[26] In Bobbitt's view, "[w]e are incapable of making something that will obviate (rather than suppress) the requirement for moral decision"[27] in constitutional law. Constitutional law is intrinsically a moral activity, just as Judge Hand understood Justice Holmes to imply. But the ethical aspect of constitutional decision making does not lie, at least not proximately, in the decision maker's conformity to extraconstitutional moral criteria ("doing justice"). The rules by which we play the constitutional-law game are not external, but (again as Holmes implied) internal to the game. Constitutional "[l]aw is something we do, not something we have as a consequence of something we do."[28] Constitutional decisions cannot be politically or ethically neutral, because the very purpose and role of constitutional law in our society is to enable people or groups to pursue goals that they choose in the light of their politics, their understanding of society, their moral beliefs, and so on. Constitutional law is, if you like the expression, politics, although people who adopt that expression as a slogan almost invariably intend it as a cynical bon mot ("it's just politics") and thereby show that they do not understand law (or politics).

The activity of constitutional law, however, is not the free-form political or ethical argument that is appropriate in a "political" forum such as a legislature. Whatever his or her goals, someone doing constitutional law must present reasons and conclusions stated in the modes of thought and discussion recognized as forms of legal argument—what Bobbitt called "the modalities of legal argument."[29] This description of constitutional argument as reasoning through the modalities is conceptual and definitional, although its historical origins lie in the founding era's relocation of sovereignty. The crucial (and novel) feature of American constitutionalism was the separation of sovereignty from the state. "If the sovereign is distinct from the government, then the instruments of state can be limited in their authority," and the idea of "a written constitution to govern a state" becomes possible. Thus, in American society questions of the constitutional structure and powers of the state have become lawyers' questions, and "the power of the state, no longer sovereign, [has been] put under law—the Constitution—and [thus] put under the common law forms of argument" that were originally and have remained what defines legal argument.[30] Something counts as a constitutional-law argument, it is a move according to the rules of the game, if it takes the form of one of the recognized modalities of argument,[31] because they are "the grammar of [constitutional] law, that system of logical constraints that the practices of legal activities have developed in our particular culture."[32]

> There is no constitutional legal argument outside these modalities. Outside these forms, a proposition about the US constitution can be a fact, or be elegant, or be amusing or even poetic, and although such assessments exist as legal statements in some possible legal world, they are not actualized in our legal world.[33]

Bobbitt's modalities are second-order descriptions of how one goes about doing constitutional law, just as the rules of grammar are second-order descriptions of the way in which those competent in the language speak and write.

Something like Bobbitt's account of constitutional-law argument is part of the game we are seeking to identify, but obedience to Bobbitt-style grammar on its own cannot answer the problem we identified at the end of the last chapter. If the rules of the constitutional-law game were simply that the justices must produce opinions using Bobbitt's grammar to "justify" results they reach on whatever grounds they think moral ("do justice," whatever you think that means), then the Constitution (or constitutional law) would be nothing but an elaborate shell game, the cover we insist that the justices provide for decisions they have reached on other grounds entirely—and this would be a surrender to Justice Johanna's cynical and instrumentalist view of constitutional law. Holmes, for one, would resist such a demeaning account of the justices' job, and Bobbitt would too.[34] But what is the response to Johanna's insistence that when she puts together an opinion that uses the proper sorts of talk she has done all that the rules of the game require?

To answer that question, we need to shift somewhat the use we are making of Justice Holmes's metaphor, away from thinking about a game's formal rules (bishops can't jump over pawns) to the notion of fair play. It may not violate a general rule of chess to engage in some sort of distracting behavior during an informal game while your opponent is deciding on her move, but a deliberate attempt to use such behavior to impair her ability to make a good decision would seem to most people unfair, an abuse of the relationship that the two players entered into when they agreed to play the game. (It might also violate tournament rules, but that puts us back in the world of the formal rules.) What is the equivalent in the constitutional-law game? What must the justices do, and not do, in order to play fair with one another and with the American Republic when they make constitutional decisions? The formal rules of the game (Bobbitt's grammar) tell one how to structure an argument that counts as constitutional law, but some of the time that leaves one free to choose which argument to advance. Constitutional law, being law, always must supply an answer to any question within its scope: in any nonacademic situation, no matter how close the question, there is a yes or no answer. Conscientious constitutional decision takes place under this mandate. We turn now to an example of an interpreter, not, as it happens, a justice, who it seems to me exemplified fair play in the choice of how to answer constitutional questions that have debatable answers, where the most one can honestly say is that a given resolution seems the most convincing.

3 ⸖ A Question of Degree

The justices of the United States Supreme Court are not, of course, the only governmental officials who write opinions on questions of constitutional interpretation. In addition to the judges of state and other federal courts, lawyers in the elected branches of American government address constitutional issues in a variety of situations and at times through formal written documents that closely resemble in format and style judicial opinions. Lacking the insulation from direct political responsibility that the Constitution deliberately affords federal judges, political-branch lawyers are, it would seem, even more poorly positioned than the justices to play the constitutional-law game fairly. Evidence that they can, and sometimes do, would go far toward making it possible to imagine that we can ask more of the Supreme Court than a justice like Johanna or even Oliver and Marsha is willing to give us. A single example may not be evidence, but in this chapter we shall consider one that I believe is highly suggestive.

In the twenty-first century the attorney general of the United States is the chief administrator of one of the great departments of the federal executive branch. His or her time is taken up largely with the duties of supervising thousands of federal attorneys and other employees and with the responsibilities of a member of the president's cabinet. It was not always so. When the first constitutional Congress created the office in 1789, the attorney general had only two statutory duties: to represent the United States before the Supreme Court and to write opinions of law at the request of the president or other high executive-branch officers. These were, furthermore, personal responsibilities, for there was no Department of Justice; indeed, before 1818 the attorney general lacked even clerical assistance, and as late as 1850 his staff consisted of one clerk and a messenger. Before the 1850s, the attorney general received a much smaller salary than that of the other members of the president's cabinet, on the expectation that he would support himself in part through private practice, an expectation that made it somewhat unclear whether the attorney general was truly an executive officer or more like retained counsel.[1] In 1870, however, acting on old suggestions, Congress created the Department of Justice, providing for an enhanced staff for the attorney general and granting him supervisory authority over other federal lawyers.

The long-term consequence of this decision was, no doubt inevitably, to make the office of attorney general an increasingly administrative and even bureaucratic one and to diminish—almost to the vanishing point by the late twentieth century—the attorney general's personal participation in his historic roles as litigator and legal adviser.[2] This shift in actual practice was a gradual one, however, and one which the 1870 Congress anticipated and sought to check by permitting the attorney general to delegate opinion writing to other departmental attorneys but requiring him to approve the opinions so delegated before issuing them; constitutional questions, the act of 1870 provided, could not be delegated.[3] Thus, although the first attorney general appointed to administer the new department, Amos T. Akerman, had duties ranging far beyond those of his predecessors, as a matter both of tradition and of statutory obligation he was still, personally, the president's legal adviser on questions of constitutional law.[4]

Late in Akerman's brief service as attorney general, President Ulysses S. Grant requested his opinion on a constitutional issue which the president himself had instigated by appointing an advisory commission on civil service reform pursuant to congressional legislation authorizing him to "prescribe . . . rules and regulations for the admission of persons into the civil service" in the interests of efficiency and professionalism. The commission took under consideration a proposal to recommend to Grant that with certain exceptions to be specified later, appointments to offices in the civil service "shall be determined by a competitive examination." The federal government had used examinations to determine the qualifications of applicants for clerks' positions since 1853; the commission's proposal broke new ground by extending the range of positions covered and by making the examination the means of choosing the successful candidate rather than of creating a pool of qualified candidates from whom the appointment could be made. It was this latter aspect of the proposal which concerned Grant.

As Akerman cannot but have known, the commission's proposal presented Grant with a potentially distasteful choice. Grant had campaigned on a platform calling for civil service reform, the commission was of his own making, a system of (ostensibly) "choosing the best person possible" had an obvious political appeal, and a strong whiff of corruption lingered about Grant's administration: informing the commission that he would not accept this proposal represented a potential political embarrassment both with the public at large and in Grant's relations with Congress. On the other hand, the presidency had been badly weakened by the bitter struggle between President Andrew Johnson, Grant's predecessor, and Congress, a struggle that led to Johnson's near removal from office and a residue of legislation intended to circumscribe the president's freedom of action. Grant was personally sensitive to this political background and made recurrent efforts over his two terms to resist congressional encroachments on his official authority. Conceding the legitimacy of a self-imposed limitation on his power of appointment could easily be seen as a precedent for legislation striking at the heart of the power—the president's discretion in deciding whom to appoint.

It would have been easy for Attorney General Akerman to address the question President Grant posed him in terms primarily political or institutional. The "real" question before the attorney general, one is tempted to say even now, involved the balance between the legislative and executive branches, a balance that Grant, and presumably Akerman (at least insofar as he was acting as the president's lawyer), believed dangerously askew because of events following the assassination of Abraham Lincoln. However much Grant might favor civil service reform, out of expedience or conviction or some mixture of the two, anything which limited the president's decisions in making appointments to federal office would strike at the heart of the president's ability to control the executive branch—his control over the personnel who actually carry out the executive tasks of government. Grant had already fought hard to undo the damage Congress had inflicted on the executive's independence when it sought to insulate presidential appointees from presidential dismissal; the commission's proposal would insulate most appointments from presidential control up front, with similarly detrimental effects on his ability to control the execution of the laws.

The commission's proposal, to be sure, was an intraexecutive matter, but Grant's authority to implement it, like his authority to create the commission in the first place, derived from the act of March 3, 1871, that Akerman quoted at the beginning of his opinion.[5] Akerman assumed, reasonably if not quite incontrovertibly, that what Congress could authorize the president to do in this regard, Congress could mandate directly. And if that were so, then conceding the president's power under the act to restrict his own discretion voluntarily meant, or arguably entailed, conceding that Congress could do so against the president's will.[6] In identifying this as the real problem to be addressed, Akerman could have written an opinion pointing out the threat such a view of Congress's powers might present to the constitutional separation of powers, and to the president's ability to fulfill his duty "to take Care that the Laws be faithfully executed": on such broad grounds, it might be concluded, the possibility of any alienation of discretion in appointments ought to be rejected. Such an opinion would not be patently wrong, or political in any invidious sense: almost a century later, an acting attorney general would quote Akerman at length in advising President Dwight D. Eisenhower that Congress could not prevent the president from exercising his discretion in making a military appointment (a matter about which Akerman himself thought there might be stronger arguments for congressional authority).[7] Basing his conclusion on general constitutional principles, furthermore, might well be thought a more persuasive and defensible approach for Akerman to take: more statesmanlike and less like that of a pettifogging lawyer. The great chief justice of the early Republic, John Marshall, was famous for his penchant for deciding constitutional questions on the broadest and most fundamental grounds, and that preference has not disappeared: a modern Supreme Court justice once chastised his colleagues, in a case involving the president's power to choose executive-branch officers, for "devot[ing] most of [their] attention to such relatively technical details as the Appointments Clause and the removal power," rather than focusing on "the concept of a government of separate and coordinate powers."[8]

Attorney General Akerman, however, did not begin with such a grand approach, but rather focused his attention, at least initially, on a series of "technical details." He began in an exquisitely lawyerly manner: restating the question the president had presented, and then narrowing it as far as possible by excluding from consideration whatever issues he could. The president's question related only to civil service positions which were "offices" in the constitutional sense;[9] it did not implicate appointments in the armed forces; there was a specific constitutional provision at issue, the appointments clause of Article II, Section 2, but also other, somewhat parallel provisions in Article I which should be taken into consideration. The result of this spadework was to enable Akerman again to restate the president's question, but this time in terms of the specific constitutional issue specifically at hand: whether

> a rule, whether prescribed by Congress, or by the President in pursuance of authority given by Congress, that a vacant civil office must be given to the person who is

found to stand foremost in a competitive examination, in effect makes the judges in that examination the appointing power to that office, and thus contravenes the constitutional provisions on the subject of appointments.

What Akerman had done up to this point was one of the most ordinary of lawyerly exercises, defining with precision the question that he had to answer. Doing so was no mere formality, however: Akerman's professional punctilio set bounds within which his answer had to abide and could be criticized. Whatever the relevance of recent political history or President Grant's call for reform, Akerman implied that they could be considered only within the context of legal argument.

Akerman began his discussion of how to resolve the question he had defined by addressing the constitutional text. Article II states that the president "shall appoint Ambassadors, other public Ministers and Consuls, Judges of the supreme Court, and all other Officers of the United States whose Appointments are not herein otherwise provided for, and which shall be established by Law." It goes on to authorize Congress by statute to vest the appointment of "inferior Officers, as they think proper, in the President alone, in the Courts of Law, or in the Heads of Departments." In every case, except those dealt with in Article I concerning the officers of the Senate and House of Representatives, the Constitution on the face of it requires that officers of the United States be appointed by some officer or entity designated by Article II for that purpose (a "constitutional depositary of that power"). Having dismissed out of hand any argument that the language of the appointments clause could be treated as nonbinding,[10] Akerman acknowledged that the language was not, as a linguistic matter, dispositive. The word "appoint" could simply refer to "a formal act, that is, merely to authenticate a selection not made by the appointing power"; if so, Akerman further conceded, then Congress is free to provide for the appointment of civil officers in any way it chooses. On the other hand, appointment might "impl[y] an exercise of judgment and will," in which case requiring the president (or any other valid "constitutional depositary" of the appointment power) to appoint the person with the highest score on an examination would make the "the will and judgment of the civil-service commission" determinative. Put another way, the words of the Constitution, which Akerman thought binding as an axiomatic matter, do not themselves resolve whether the "appointing power conferred in the Constitution [is] a substantial [or] merely a nominal function." Fidelity to the words of the text had driven him beyond the bare text (and the dictionary).

It would be surprising for someone to set up a contrast between giving a constitutional provision "a substantial" or "merely a nominal" significance and then to adopt the latter, but Akerman did not rely solely on clever word choices to support his conclusion that "I cannot but believe that the judgment and will of the constitutional depositary of that power should be exercised in every appointment." Instead, he offered President Grant two reasons why the Constitution's language about appointments ought to be given "a substantial" reading. He first invoked "the reasons for the constitutional provision." The "makers of the Constitution," he argued, had concluded "after careful consideration . . . that in no other depositaries of it could the judgment and will to make proper appointments so certainly be found" because of the knowledge, ability, and sense of responsibility they expected the president, department heads, and federal judges to possess; echoing a repeated theme in the *Federalist* papers and elsewhere, Akerman added that the Constitution "placed the power in the hands of those who would have a particular interest in using it well." Akerman's presentation of this argument for his position reads a little oddly to a modern lawyer, accustomed as we are to elaborate citations and proof texts, but the substance of his assertions about the original purpose of the appointments clause was unremarkable, being a substantive paraphrase of Hamilton's discussion in *The Federalist*, numbers 76 and 77, and of Justice Story's analysis of the clause's intended purposes in his great treatise on the Constitution.[11]

Akerman's second reason for giving "appoint" substantive meaning rested on the implications of not doing so for the Senate's role in the appointments process. As he noted, the "most important civil appointments are made by the President, with the advice and consent of the Senate" (the appointments clause, recall, permits other arrangements only with respect to "inferior Officers"). But "[i]f Congress can compel the President to nominate a person selected by others, it can compel the Senate to advise and consent to the nomination"; the Senate's role stands on no higher textual plane than the president's, and if one is subject to congressional dimunition, so is the other. In addition to disregarding, again, the original purpose of "the constitutional design"—"that the judgment of the Senate shall revise the judgment of the President, and that the judgment of both shall concur in filling the office"—such a conclusion, Akerman believed, failed to make sense out of the words of the clause: "advice and consent imply an exercise of judgment and will."[12] A broad-brush, general-principles answer to the question troubling Grant might well have missed what Akerman's technical approach did not, that the underlying constitutional issue was not a simple bipolar confrontation between executive and legislative power, but involved a complex set of constitutional arrangements in which the proper roles of president, Senate, and Congress as a whole were at stake.

Having laid out, succinctly but clearly, the affirmative case for his affirmative answer to Grant's question, Akerman turned to possible objections, which he treated at some length. His discussion of past practice is of special interest. "The legislation of the country from an early period," he wrote, "has been supposed to authorize a different constitutional view from that which is herein expressed," and he immediately conceded that the Supreme Court had only recently observed that a "practical construction of the Constitution by Congress . . . is entitled to great consideration, and should be followed in all cases of doubt."[13] Briskly reviewing the history of legislation with appointments issues, Akerman noted a way in which apparent exercises of congressional control over appointments could be distinguished, but he concluded with a candid admission that "some of them [the antecedent is "legislative precedents"] take for granted that Congress is absolute in the matter of appointments." The admission made, Akerman denied its importance: "But such ... is not the constitutional rule." The "legislative precedents," if taken as determinative, would authorize Congress to vest the appointment power itself, whether "substantial" or "nominal," elsewhere than in the constitutional depositaries listed in the text. Earlier attorneys general had repeatedly rejected that proposition, and a recent Supreme Court decision supported their position.[14] Even Congress, he observed sardonically, "appears to have" agreed "when its attention was called to the subject." The supposed "practical construction of the Constitution" in earlier legislation was indefensible as a reading of the text and thus can provide no support for a claim that Congress can bind the discretion of the constitutional appointing power to choose a particular individual based on an examination or, indeed, any other criterion.

Akerman turned finally to a subsidiary question which the civil service commission had presented: would it be lawful for the president, acting under the March 1871 act, to "regulate the exercise of the appointing power now vested in the heads of Departments, or in the courts of law, so as to restrict appointments to a class of persons whose qualifications or fitness shall have been determined by an examination," in other words, to limit the pool of possible appointees to applicants who showed that they met a competence threshold determined by a presidentially ordained examination? To do so would be to circumscribe, to some extent, the discretion of the appointing power; once again, to concede that the president could take this action pursuant to congressional authorization seemed, to Akerman, clearly to pose the question of whether Congress could do so directly, and against the president's will. Since he thought the "very ample authority" conferred by the act would encompass such a rule, the constitutional question could not be avoided.

But on this issue, Akerman came to a different conclusion. The fatal flaw in requiring an appointment to go to the candidate with the highest score on a test is that there is nothing left for the appointing power to do but rubber-stamp the decision of the test's examiners: the only judgment and will involved would be those of the examiners. But the use of criteria to identify a class of people qualified for a position, from among whom the appointing power may then choose, is a different matter. That power—whichever of the constitutional possibilities it might be—"would still have a reasonable scope for its own judgment and will." To be sure, it could be "argued that a right in Congress to limit in the least the field of selection, implies a right to carry on the contracting process to the designation of a particular individual. But I do not think this a fair conclusion." Constitutional law, law generally, Akerman told Grant, is frequently not a matter of binary choices, in which there is either a bright, incontrovertible line between X and not-X or no line at all:

> But it may be asked, at what point must the contracting process stop? I confess my inability to answer. But the difficulty of drawing a line between such limitations as are, and such as are not, allowed by the Constitution, is no proof that both classes do not exist. In constitutional and legal inquiries, right or wrong is often a question of degree. Yet it is impossible to tell precisely where in the scale right ceases and wrong begins. Questions of excessive bail, cruel punishments, excessive damages, and reasonable doubts are familiar instances.

It is at this point in his opinion that Attorney General Akerman acknowledges most clearly the moral aspect of constitutional decision making. In the highly technical appointments clause issue he was considering, just as in the familiar issues of *excessive* bail and damages, *cruel* punishments, *reasonable* doubts, someone charged with interpreting the Constitution cannot avoid the task of answering questions that have no determinate answers before they are decided, that are by their very nature debatable. It does not follow, however, that the Constitution must be interpreted as a simple blank check. Good faith in interpretation must, at a minimum, take the Constitution seriously as an authority, as the goal toward which the interpreter aims.

Akerman was quite aware of, and quite honest about, the implication of this perspective, which is that constitutional interpreters and constitutional actors alike must act in good faith ("In the matter now in question, it is not supposable that Congress or the President would require of candidates for office qualifications unattainable by a sufficient number to afford ample room for choice"), using their best judgment both to ascertain the constitutional rule and to apply it, in situations where there may be no logically demonstrable "right" answer. Treating constitutional issues as questions of technical law sometimes drives us beyond the realm of professional expertise and algorithmic reasoning—"I confess my inability to answer"—to a sphere in which intellectual and moral integrity are essential.

←

The specific question which President Grant posed to Attorney General Akerman is hardly on the top of anyone's list of the twenty-first century's most burning constitutional issues. And yet I think there is much to learn from Akerman's opinion that is of the utmost importance for contemporary constitutional law, and in particular about what it might mean to play the constitutional-law game fairly.

Let us begin with what may well be a burning question (or set of questions) for any reader patient enough to make it this far: What is the point of examining, in some detail, a mid-nineteenth-century legal opinion by a long-dead attorney general? Wasn't the answer Akerman gave Grant foreordained, a translation into law talk of Grant's political preferences? Indeed, what else could a "legal" opinion by a lawyer serving at the will of a political master be? Isn't this part of the reason why, to quote Chief

Justice Hughes again, "the Constitution is what the judges say it is," because judges, unlike lawyers in the "political" branches, are neutral, dispassionate expositors of the law rather than advocates? (Quick note: I will drop the scare quotes around "political" after this, but the reader should keep in mind that all I mean by the adjective is to distinguish the two branches of the federal government which are electorally responsible from the one that isn't, or not directly.) Although the more sophisticated the lawyer, the more nuanced the expression, I suspect that a great many members of the profession, and doubtless many other Americans as well, share the assumption of a sharp dichotomy between judges and other governmental lawyers which underlies all this.[15] And that assumption, in turn, fuels the assumption that documents like Akerman's opinion—unlike judicial opinions—cannot be taken seriously as opinions of constitutional *law*.

The problem with this dichotomy—judges good, politicians and their legal eagles bad—is that it combines an extreme cynicism about the political branches of government (and often all branches of state government) with an extreme credulity, in practice if not always in theory, about the federal judiciary. Both sides of this coin are gross exaggerations of whatever truth they may contain. The history of the Republic is replete with examples of government lawyers working in the political branches who took positions which were not mere translations of their superiors' wishes into legalese, and to say this is to risk ignoring the possibility and the historical reality of principled obedience to the law on the part of those superiors. The history of the Republic is equally replete with examples of courts coming to debatable decisions which, as it just so happened, accorded with the political (moral, economic, whatever) preferences of the judges. Judges, even good judges, do not lose their political perspectives when they go on the bench; political-branch lawyers, except for knaves, do not lose their integrity when they accept public office (and if knaves—like Justice John—it is not their office that has deprived them of integrity). Whatever the relative distribution of authority over constitutional interpretation ought to be between the political branches and the judiciary, it cannot rest on a sharp distinction between the political and the apolitical nature of the officials themselves.

But there remains a distinction or dichotomy that is embedded deeply in American constitutional law. Constitutional interpreters, in any government position or out of it, are (in John Marshall's words) "so much influenced by the wishes, the affections and the general theories" they hold that their disagreements over constitutional questions will often reflect their conflicting political commitments.[16] And yet no constitutional interpreter in the American system ever asserts that her answer to a constitutional question is a political as opposed to a legal one. At least for the purposes for which governmental officials, including judges, discuss constitutional meaning, the Constitution is axiomatically assumed to be law, and constitutional judgments are assumed to involve attention to this law, which is assumed to be somewhat apart from, and not to be identified with, the moral or policy preferences of the interpreter. When Attorney General Akerman wrote that "[s]uch, however, is not the constitutional rule," he did not expect President Grant to understand his assertion to be translatable as "such, however, is not what I (or you) would think best for the administration, the executive branch, or even the country." As we shall see, arguments about what is best in some sense often play a perfectly legitimate role in constitutional argument, but that form of argument is not reducible simply to the assertion of what the "interpreter" thinks the better outcome. Interpretation, at least in the American constitutional tradition, implies the existence of something which is to be interpreted.

Just under the surface in Akerman's opinion, furthermore, is his assumption, again one shared, I think, generally in our tradition, that there is more to constitutional law than putting one's views in a proper form. Akerman did not deny the status of "constitutional" or "legal" reasoning to the arguments he rejected. The problem with arguing for the constitutionality of the civil service commission's proposal on the ground of general principle (it is dictated by the separation of powers), practical precedent (Congress has done similar things before), or un-workability (any other view requires one to draw unprincipled lines) was not, in his view, that these were not legitimate legal arguments, but rather that they were not *persuasive* ones or, better, the *most persuasive* ones. Akerman thought, and sought to persuade Grant, that on balance there were better arguments for the other view. The argument from the general concept of divided powers lost sight of the complex nature of the arrangements actually ordained by the Constitution's text. Congress's practice was mixed in import and if taken literally led to conclusions no one would accept. However hard in practice the line drawing might be, it was no different in principle from exercises everyone would agree the law required, and thus had to be possible for a constitutional interpreter acting in good faith. Of course none of these arguments, in the end, required acquiescence as a matter of logical or geometric proof. President Grant might well read them, think about them, and conclude that he did not accept them. That possibility is implicit in Akerman's admission that "I confess my inability to answer" the question where to draw the line between legitimate congressional dictation of qualifications and unconstitutional congressional dictation of the candidate to appoint. By definition, any conclusion about the validity of a particular congressional requirement would be subject to quarrel unless it was so far to one side of the spectrum that arguing would be specious. But that did not lead Akerman, as we have seen, to the conclusion that no line could be drawn as a matter of constitutional law. Where there is room for rational argument, he realized, issues of constitutional interpretation are proper matters for persuasion rather than proof, and none the worse, or less lawlike, for that fact.

We are now at the point of asking ourselves how Attorney General Akerman could view his task in answering President Grant's question. Simply telling Grant (in legal gobblydegook) what the president wanted to hear would not in fact respond to

Grant's inquiry, however much it might address Grant's preferences. But coherent constitutional-law arguments could be
made to support either conclusion. So what to do? The answer
I have already intimated is that Akerman ought to have seen his
job as one of advancing the most persuasive argument, as indeed
he did. But that only raises two further problems: how does one
know what is the most, or more, persuasive argument, and why
should one adopt it in the first place?

As to persuasiveness, Akerman's practice gives us some clues.
One feature of his opinion that I hope has become clear is his care
and craft. Akerman shared Justice Frankfurter's concern to write
legal arguments that would attract professional approval. Akerman loved his profession, and there is every reason to think he took
a craftsman's pride in getting it right, or as right as he could. There
is no single, logically incontestable way for an ironsmith to make a
garden gate, but even a layman or -woman can tell the difference
between excellent workmanship and the slipshod or hasty. The
same is true with law, and Akerman's opinion, I believe, shows his
concern to do excellent legal work: defining the issues, identifying
the relevant authorities, treating them with honesty and insight,
avoiding the non sequitur and other logical flaws, putting the
argument in forms available to the reader. In the absence of craft,
a constitutional-law argument is beneath consideration.

Closely allied to this concern, indeed part of it although use-
fully treated separately, is candor. Akerman was honest with Grant.
Whatever failings we might find now in his opinion (I myself see
few, if any), I think it clear that his goal was to give the president
the ability to make his, Grant's, own judgment about the persuasiveness of Akerman's reasoning, neither hiding the ball nor
playing verbal games with the issues. In doing so, Akerman made
of constitutional law, in this particular and small instance, something open rather than closed, an enterprise of making sense to
others rather than of dictating to them. Rather than obfuscating
the problems attendant on giving an answer to Grant's question,
or laying claim to a certainty that he could not truthfully possess, Akerman engaged in what James Boyd White calls "living

speech," legal argument that reveals the speaker's mind at work in attempting to resolve the question before him. That did not mean that Akerman was dismissing the role of legal knowledge and ability in answering the question Grant posed—far from it; the fact that Grant asked the question was an acknowledgement that there is a role for professional expertise in constitutional matters. The Constitution is law. But it is law which is not the exclusive preserve of the experts and bears authority only insofar as it persuades others. Without intellectual candor, a constitutional-law argument can only trick; it cannot persuade.[17] In this respect Akerman's opinion is very different from the cynical and manipulative opinions that are all Justices John and Johanna can write. To the extent that Justices Oliver and Marsha fall into self-deception or the repetition of positions that they cannot consistently hold, their opinions, too, fail to be living speech of the sort Akerman exemplifies.

Persuasion in a constitutional-law argument, furthermore, depends on the extent to which the interpreter seems, to the reader (or hearer), to grasp the point of the constitutional enterprise. At the heart of Akerman's reasoning was his insistence that the Constitution's provisions relating to appointments have a purpose. They are not simply formal arrangements (it has to be done some way or the other), and they are not to be construed as aimed at now-obsolete objectives from the founding era (an example being the idea that involving the Senate in appointments enables the gentry to override plebeian or populist appointments). Akerman grounded his own argument in an interpretation of the purposes of "the makers of the Constitution," but his reasoning is not fundamentally backward looking: his invocations of the founders are as much invitations to Grant to ask where we should go as they are invitations to ask where our ancestors may have been. In part Akerman is persuasive—or not—to the extent that he seems to the reader to make sense of the American constitutional experiment.[18]

Attorney General Ackerman, in answering President Grant's inquiry, assumed that the Constitution is, or gives rise to, law in a technical sense, the sort of human practice in which there is a role for technical expertise, learning, and skill which are not common among any citizen body as a whole. But his own practice, while technically skilled, was aimed at allowing those lacking the relevant professional training (Grant was a soldier, not a lawyer) to understand and indeed to judge his professional judgment. We shall return to the paradox in action this creates later; for now our interest is in a more immediate concern, why one should ever treat constitutional questions as ones of technical law. The Constitution, as we have usually understood it across its more than two centuries of existence, is not a collection of, or a reference to, general concepts about divided government, individual liberty, and so on. It is, rather, a set of specific rules (some, to be sure, very broad and open textured), and the answer to constitutional questions must therefore begin with a close consideration of the rules. The rules may be read to reflect or embody broader themes, of course—this book reads the Constitution in just that manner—but it is the rules, the words of the text, which are ultimately determinative of any constitutional dispute. And that presents a rather obvious difficulty: what is the interpreter to do when she finds a conflict between the best reading of the words and what she thinks on other grounds is the superior "constitutional" outcome? If, as I asserted a moment ago, there is a point to the constitutional enterprise, why should that point be lost because the makers of the Constitution's text used clumsy or maladroit language, or even because they did not see as clearly as we do what the implications of its point in fact are? And the point can be broadened: why should a technical lawyer's argument about the meaning of the Constitution, whether based on the wording or on other considerations, ever prevail against a view that is more attractive politically, morally, or socially?

It is possible, of course, to respond to these questions by embracing the view that "the Constitution" is, in fact, the set of all those answers to constitutional questions which are the best for the American community, politically, morally, and socially. The distinguished constitutional scholar Henry Monaghan calls this the "perfect Constitution" thesis;[19] it is clearly Justice Marsha's view. Allowing those answers to give way to technical argument is a bizarre fetishism, a refusal to allow the Constitution and the Republic to be the best they can be, and an unnecessary refusal at that: the language of the Constitution is so open, and the tools of legal reasoning so flexible, that it is a poor lawyer who cannot "prove" that the politically best answer is also the "constitutional" one. There are, to be sure, some hard nuts to crack—it is difficult to make much that is attractive out of Article IV, Section 2, Clause 3 (the fugitive slave clause)[20]—but there is nothing in either text or legal argument to preclude someone's adopting a conclusion that is defensible morally. Nothing, that is, except the concept of integrity which Attorney General Akerman evoked at the end of his opinion. It is possible to write out arguments which use the language of constitutional law to come to whatever results one prefers, and it is equally possible for someone with very different views to do exactly the same thing. We do not all agree, as a people, on the set of best answers to questions of governmental authority and individual liberty, and if the ultimate criterion is, simply and always, what the interpreter thinks best, in some extraconstitutional sense, there will be as many different "Constitutions" as there are conflicting interpreters. The perfect-Constitution view is ultimately incoherent because it evacuates the Constitution itself of meaning and collapses constitutional law into the sort of government by judicial choice that I claimed, in the preface, is not the general understanding of constitutionalism in our society.

We can now, I think, begin to see why Attorney General Akerman thought it better to deal with President Grant's question as one requiring the exercise of professional and technical judgment, and more generally why our tradition has insisted on treating the Constitution as the object of professional and technical argument. In a community which is deeply divided along political, ideological, and ethical lines, technical argument provides something which we share in common. It serves as a sort of constitutional lingua franca, a means of communication which transcends the heated disagreements which it serves to express. But technical law can perform this role only if it is something other than a mere tool, the rhetorical clothing in which predetermined outcomes are dressed up so they will be respectable. If that is all that is going on, then professional discourse *is* (or becomes) a means of obfuscation, and we might well dispense with it. Akerman's example suggests that there is an alternative, that technical argument can be undertaken in good faith, with a commitment to weighing, in a fair-minded way, all of the relevant professional considerations. Akerman did not deny, of course, what Marshall had seen long before, that even a good-faith effort to interpret the Constitution will often be shaped by the interpreter's other beliefs and commitments, but he clearly believed that there is something more to constitutional *interpretation* than dress-up. By casting his own reasoning in the terms and methods of technical law, Akerman rendered his opinion open to Grant, or anyone else, to evaluate the persuasiveness of that reasoning within a framework that is the common possession of the community rather than the sectarian perspective of a faction.[21]

↵

Several observations follow from our examination of Attorney General Akerman's opinion on the civil service commission issue. One is that Akerman thought of his role as a political-branch lawyer as one bound by ethical considerations: he was obliged, in answering President Grant's question, to play the game according to the rules, just as the justices are. It doesn't follow, and Akerman didn't claim, that the rules are exactly the same for a public lawyer acting in his, rather than a judge's, role. To deny any distinction between the (political) decisions of a political-branch lawyer and the (law-observing) decisions of a judge simply isn't plausible as a pragmatic matter or acceptable normatively. This point is not always self-evident, for the deep

dualism in American thought about law and politics has created two schools of thought on the role of the political-branch
lawyer. On the one hand are those who assimilate the public
lawyer to the common image of private counsel as primarily the
servant of the client, not of the law. As one commentator has
asserted, no doubt quite accurately, the ordinary president "expects his attorney general . . . to be his advocate rather than an
impartial arbiter, a judge of the legality of his action." Taking
this view to its logical extreme, the lawyer for the government
should not be expected to profess any genuine loyalty to the
law: she is, and her words and deeds should be interpreted as
those of, a partisan. There is on this view no real problem of ten-
sion between law and politics for the political-branch lawyer,
because his true allegiance is to politics and his relationship to
law is purely instrumental.

The opposite view is held by those who believe that public
lawyers, like judges, are above all called to put loyalty to the law
above any commitment to the politics of the administration in
which they serve. In recent years this perspective has been asso-
ciated in particular with the office of the United States solicitor
general—a book popular some years ago called that officer "the
tenth justice"[22]—but the image of the public lawyer as a quasi-
judicial figure is often applied quite broadly. Many descriptions
of President Gerald Ford's distinguished attorney general, Edward Levi, capture this image: "He is not a partisan. He is be-
holden to no one. For too long politics has been permitted to
intrude into the Justice Department." Levi provided "thoughtful, nonpolitical and highly principled leadership." (Note how
that sentence juxtaposes and almost equates the "highly principled" with the "nonpolitical.") Levi himself stated his ambition to "make clear, by word and deed, that our law is not an
instrument of partisan purpose."[23] This view of the political-
branch lawyer as apolitical shares the same nobility of purpose
as the ideal of the apolitical judge, and it suffers from the same
problems. The problems are exacerbated by the fact that unlike
federal judges, political-branch lawyers, at least high-ranking

ones, are as an institutional matter clearly within the realm of the political.

The law/politics dichotomy, then, produces, even more clearly for political-branch lawyers than for judges, a debilitating and ultimately unworkable split between different aspects of their job. Such lawyers spend much of our time advising political officials how those officials can achieve their policy goals within the bounds of the law. A second important task consists in predicting how the courts, and sometimes the public, will evaluate the lawfulness of proposed action by Congress or the executive branch. Perhaps most important, the lawyers within the legislative and executive branches regularly address questions of lawfulness per se.

None of the activities I've just mentioned can be done well—none of them ultimately can be done at all—if politics is truly to be excluded from the undertaking. The tracing of a satisfactory path to a policy objective through lawful means is often fraught with choices that are themselves political and moral in nature, and the task often requires that the lawyer share the objective, at least for the purpose of devising and providing advice. Accurate prediction about whether other governmental entities or the public will accept the lawfulness of a proposed action or policy depends in part on informed and ultimately political judgment about how other individuals will balance the inherent issues of law, policy, and partisanship. And as Attorney General Akerman's political-branch lawyers, so the high Court's justices sometimes encounter questions of law that have no determinate answer based on the legal materials narrowly construed and that as a result require the interpreter to go beyond those materials to the deeper moral commitments of the American political order. Unlike judges, moreover, lawyers who serve in the political branches cannot displace political responsibility for their legal conclusions in the name of judicial deference to democratic choice and to elected officials—considerations that by definition do not apply to someone who is not a judge and who is ultimately responsible to elected officials who exercise power by virtue of democratic choice. Politics is inseparable from public lawyering for Congress or the president.

At the same time, effective public lawyering is not simply politics, or advocacy for politicians. The politics that is inseparable from public lawyering is not mere partisanship, nor is its purpose to advance the personal fortunes of the officials who are the public lawyer's immediate "clients." Public lawyers are called to be lawyers, not campaign workers or even policy analysts. Let me illustrate. Even the most brazen political officer in our culture scarcely can assert that the law places no limits on his or her discretion to act. Implicit in the political question How can we achieve this goal? is the awareness that law or, if you please, the people's understanding of the law is going to channel any plausible response. (Recall that the Supreme Court's decisions are limited by what is socially and politically plausible.) And ultimately, although politicians do not like being told no, to an extent perhaps surprising to those outside government, they are unwilling to act against legal advice. They expect to be told if the legal justifications for a proposed action or policy are implausible. The political-branch lawyer who views law as nothing more than a set of rhetorical tools to be used in whatever manner necessary to serve his or her political masters is an unsatisfactory servant in the long run. One cannot engage successfully in the tasks of the political-branch lawyer simply by saying what will satisfy the policy maker who asked the question in the short term. To do her political job, the public lawyer must find some way to be loyal to the law.

A political-branch lawyer like Attorney General Akerman is thus in much the same quandary as a Supreme Court justice: there is no way to exclude politics in the sense I am using that term, by technique or by moral effort, and yet the very shape of her tasks assumes that law is not simply politics. But this problem in fact displays the close parallel between that lawyer's role and the task of the justices. On the pragmatic level, we have repeatedly seen that the justices of the Supreme Court appear, quite incontrovertibly, to reflect in their decisions their individual political and ideological preferences. However we are to describe the justices' job, it is not one that is hermetically sealed off from the political, the ideological, or the moral. This is not to say that the justices ought to be adherents of Justice Johanna's instrumentalism, but it does go a long way toward demolishing the wall between judges and other public lawyers that might seem implicit in my general focus in this book on decisions by the Supreme Court. And no one thinks that political-branch lawyering is insulated in general from the politics that drive the policy makers the lawyers advise and defend. There should not be, one might conclude, all that much difference in outcome and, perhaps, in moral obligation between the lawyer who wears judicial robes and the one who serves the president or Congress. Our enterprise in this essay is not limited to the duties of the justices of the high Court: others may have similar responsibilities in carrying out *their* jobs (remember Holmes!). Academics often think about the role of law in the light of a fundamental fear and dislike of the political, of the world of passion, interest, disagreement, struggle, compromise, choice. But that is the only public world that exists. Judges, including the justices of the Supreme Court, are not free of the biases and commitments it creates, and by the same token political-branch lawyers are not solely the tools of its passions. Whatever the rules of the game are, they cannot be ones that depend entirely on the peculiar privileges or tasks of judicial-branch officers. The constitutional-law game has many players.

Attorney General Akerman's handling of the question put to him suggests a second point. Akerman admirably and explicitly conceded that he had come to a constitutional decision in the teeth of responsible disagreement. "I confess my inability to answer," Akerman admitted in response to the anticipated critique that he could not draw a clear line between constitutional and unconstitutional infringements on the president's free choice in appointing officers. The point is not specific. Constitutional law is not, in controversial questions, a matter of applying algorithms that generate incontrovertible answers, even when the questions to be answered fall within a settled area of law.[24]

When it is not, it demands of the constitutional decision maker, whether judge or political-branch official, a judgment that can be governed only by conscience, by a dutiful attempt to resolve the conflict of constitutional provisions, interests, and principles as seems most proper to the decision maker. In the absence of definitive answers delivered by commonly admitted forms of arguments, the constitutional decision maker, whether judge or other public official, must come to a moral conclusion that cannot be, by definition, anything other than a question of degree, weighing the metaphorical balance between the conflicting interests. Such an activity, since it is by definition a matter of non-algorithmic judgment, is governed by considerations of fair play, in Holmes's imagery, or not at all. I have argued that Attorney General Akerman's civil service commission opinion reveals a mind and conscience struggling to answer fairly a constitutional question and doing so with admirable success. But that was one mind, one question. We need a more general description of the characteristics a constitutional decision maker ought to display. What is the shape of a constitutional conscience?

4 ⇜ Men and Women of Goodwill

On the last page of his justly famous 1982 book *After Virtue*, the philosopher Alasdair MacIntyre summed up his argument that Western society has become morally incoherent by drawing a parallel between the present day and "the epoch in which the Roman empire declined into the Dark Ages":

> A crucial turning point in that earlier history occurred when men and women of good will turned aside from the task of shoring up the Roman imperium and ceased to identify the continuation of civility and moral community with the maintenance of that imperium. What they set themselves to achieve instead . . . was the construction of new forms of community within which the moral life could be sustained so that both morality and civility might survive the coming ages of barbarism and darkness. If my account of our moral condition is correct, we ought also to conclude that for some time now we too have reached that turning point.[1]

Attempting to maintain Western social and political institutions, MacIntyre appears to have thought, is not only a hopeless effort but a perverse one, a form of service to a new barbarism that sits among the shattered remains of an earlier ethical tradition and makes of those institutions a tool for endless, irresolvable conflict. Those committed to a vision of human life that is decent, humane, civilized ought to give up as irretrievably corrupted the forms of Western common life.

MacIntyre did not leave any doubt about where he would locate American constitutional law in this account: for him, the Supreme Court's constitutional role is necessarily limited to the prevention of out-and-out civil war by ad hoc and amoral compromise. The Court is shoring up our imperium rather than maintaining our nonexistent moral community. Earlier in his book he wrote that in morally controversial cases, "[t]he Supreme Court . . . play[s] the role of a peacemaking or truce-keeping body by negotiating its way through an impasse of conflict, not by invoking our shared moral first principles. For our society as a whole has none."[2] A morally serious justice or other constitutional decision maker, in MacIntyre's opinion, cannot carry out his or her constitutional role as anything other than an effort to stave off conflict, although MacIntyre's own metaphor of truce keeping seems somewhat odd: a mediator between warring factions can have as his goal keeping the peace at all costs, making no effort to resolve the substantive disagreement between the factions. But in any event, constitutional decision making is a different sort of activity: the decision maker cannot prescind from choosing a substantive outcome (at least much of the time), and as long as American society in general accepts the role of the Supreme Court encapsulated in the strong Rule of Five, the justices can choose any number of different outcomes without serious risk of social violence. But if MacIntrye's account is correct, how can a justice pick between incommensurate values other than by simply taking sides with one of the "rival social groups adhering to rival and incompatible principles of justice" before the Court? The practice of constitutional law has no moral content beyond the avoidance of conflict, and gives no shape to the process of choosing a "constitutional" outcome other than to dictate the formalities of how the opinion should look. If someone participates in such an ethically vacuous system, will she not simply fall into the same trap of self-referential "moral" assertion that has gripped American society as a whole, and thus lose her claim to be motivated by either goodwill or civility?

I believe that Professor MacIntyre was wrong to think that American constitutional law does not and indeed cannot generate a code of civility, a set of virtues, that define and inform fair play in constitutional decision making. Implicit in the shared, social understanding of what such decision making entails is a portrait of what ethical constraints ought to inform a constitutional decision maker, that limn out the picture of someone who is playing the constitutional-law game fairly.[3] Contrary to what MacIntyre's remarks seem to imply, it is possible to describe how a constitutionally virtuous justice would approach her task.[4] The activity of interpreting and applying the Constitution, as that activity is traditionally and customarily understood, demands certain habits of mind and will—certain intellectual and moral virtues, to use the old word—of those who undertake it. The constitutional virtues, as I shall call them, are necessary if one is to engage in those political and legal practices that revolve around the Constitution. Where the constitutional virtues are imperfectly realized—no doubt most or all of the time—our practices are only partly successful. In the complete absence or eclipse of the constitutional virtues, those practices would indeed become unintelligible, just as MacIntyre suggests. But the constitutional virtues are not merely prerequisites to engaging successfully in a certain set of activities, without more general significance, in the way, say, that the habit of keeping track of the cards played is a prerequisite to being successful at playing bridge. They are virtues in the broader sense and involve choices about who we are and who we wish to be as moral actors. Whether we are actively interpreting the Constitution or are making the correlative decision to accept and obey a constitutional interpretation propounded by someone else, we are inevitably shaping ourselves as moral actors generally. And it is in that fact that we can discern why someone might think the Constitution, or the enterprise of constitutional law, to lead to the sort of practice that men and women of civility might engage in and regard as admirable. The Constitution's authority lies in the very habits of mind and will that our practices demand we develop in order that the Constitution may be interpreted. The constitutional virtues are morally worthy ambitions for citizens of a republic that is both free and inclusive.

Much rides at this point on the notion of virtue. In recent decades, the concept of the virtues has come to assume a central place in a great deal of philosophical and theological work in ethics.[5] I cannot stop to review that fascinating development, nor do I want to tie my proposal about the constitutional virtues to a particular theoretical account of the virtues, or indeed to any general need to accept virtue ethics at all. In typical academic-lawyer fashion, I simply want to raid other people's thinking for a couple of ideas useful to my own project. By a virtue, as I have already suggested, I mean a habit or disposition of mind or will, oriented in (say) Aristotelian thought to happiness or eudaimonia, and in the American constitutional tradition to the interpretation and application of the Constitution as supreme law. In addition, I am going to assume that virtues necessarily rest on presuppositions about the individuals and communities that embrace them. Aristotle, for example, presupposed that human beings, or perhaps some human beings, are political by nature, that they are, appropriately, the inhabitants of a polis. The Constitution of the United States, and the constitutional tradition of which it is the center, also make certain presuppositions about American society, even if implicitly, and the constitutional virtues are grounded in these presuppositions.[6]

Let me begin with what is, I think, the most fundamental presupposition of the Constitution: its own intelligibility. The enterprise of creating and continuing to talk over time about a written Constitution as ongoing law assumes that human beings are capable of employing language in such a fashion as to enable themselves and others to make sense of it. The point may seem obvious but it is extremely important. There are, of course, other ways in which linguistic activity can be meaningful: Tolstoy was terribly frustrated by the pleasure many contemporaneous Russian peasants took in reciting the Nicene Creed, because he thought (no doubt correctly in general) that the philosophical and theological themes of the creed were unintelligible to them. Even if Tolstoy was right, it doesn't follow, as he seems to have believed, that the peasants were acting irrationally: the meaningfulness for them of reciting the creed, in that case, lay not in its cognitive content but elsewhere.

The meaningfulness of the Constitution, on the other hand, is inextricably tied up with its cognitive content, with the intelligibility of its commands. In the American system, Chief Justice John Marshall famously wrote, "[t]he powers of the legislature are defined, and limited; and that those limits may not be mistaken, or forgotten, the constitution is written." The very purpose of the written Constitution, in other words, is to supply rules of law that we can make sense of cognitively. In discussing the implications of the judiciary's express power to decide cases arising under the Constitution, Marshall insisted that it was ridiculous to assume such a case "should be decided without examining the instrument under which it arises"; in reaching a decision, "the constitution must be looked into by the judges" for its meaning as an intelligible communication, not invoked by them as a symbol or talisman of power. When American governmental officials bind themselves "to support" the Constitution, they are not swearing blind obedience to some form or process of arbitrary decision. They are, as Marshall explained, making a promise to engage their "abilities and understanding" in a serious effort to make sense of an instrument that is susceptible to such efforts.

In his opinion in *Marbury v. Madison*, from which I have just quoted, Chief Justice Marshall had in view the Constitution as a written document, but the Constitution is more than just the words of the text. As Justice Holmes wrote in *Missouri v. Holland*, the constitutional text is a set of words that are also a constituent act, and the interpretation of the words as a linguistic matter cannot be disentangled from the interpretation of the political and legal enterprise that the words constitute.[7] As we have already seen, constitutional interpretation is not, and cannot be, done out of a dictionary. And this implies a further aspect to the presupposition of intelligibility: the Constitution presupposes that people can talk meaningfully about the purposes and goals of the American project. Such talk, as we saw in the last chapter, is intrinsically laden with political and moral content, and fraught with the possibility—the certainty at times—of deep and principled disagreement among those carrying on the discussion. But unless we assume that meaningful conversation can take place in such circumstances, American constitutional interpretation as socially understood is impossible.[8]

The constitutional virtue that flows most directly from the constitutional presupposition of intelligibility is faith. I should immediately concede that this terminological choice may seem provocative. Faith has certainly long been seen in the Western ethical tradition as a possible virtue, but it has usually been classed as a theological virtue and thus peculiar to certain sectarian strands of Western religion. I want to employ the term "faith" nevertheless, not so much to be provocative as to draw on the dual meaning it has often been given by Christian theologians: faith as the intellectual activity of belief, and faith as the practical activity of commitment. The constitutional virtue of faith—and here the reader can put the theologians to one side—involves both an acceptance of the Constitution's intelligibility (it is not just an empty vessel into which we can pour whatever values or preferences we choose) and an undertaking to govern oneself as a constitutional actor in accordance with the Constitution's intelligible meaning. Without this belief and commitment, American constitutionalism makes no sense. Indeed, law as a whole would make no sense, as Joseph Vining has persuasively argued.[9]

In an era when many academics believe that this is all moonshine or bad faith, it is worth recalling that the great intellectual antagonists of the Warren Court, Hugo Black and John Marshall Harlan, were alike in their possession of faith in the sense I am using the word. I don't mean, of course, that they didn't disagree much of the time, which they most assuredly did. Justice Black was famous for his insistence that in exercising the power of judicial review the Court's commission begins and ends with the words of the written Constitution: "no law" in the Constitution means no law, the Court should enforce only the written guarantees of the Bill of Rights and not those freedoms thought implicit in ordered liberty, and so on.[10] Justice Harlan, in contrast, thought far more in terms of interpreting the ongoing constitutional enterprise.[11] For Black, the Constitution's words necessarily embodied what are sometimes rather stark meanings: the First Amendment says "Congress shall make no law," no law means no law, and the validity under the amendment of a governmental action depends entirely on whether the action is within or without the ambit of the areas covered by the no-law command. For Harlan, in contrast, " liberty is not a series of isolated points pricked out in terms of the taking of property; the freedom of speech, press, and religion; the right to keep and bear arms . . . and so on. It is a rational continuum which, broadly speaking, includes a freedom from all substantial arbitrary impositions and purposeless restraints." Black and Harlan disagreed radically, but they disagreed radically about the best approach to carrying out a task about which in an even deeper sense they shared a common understanding. Contrary to what is often thought, Black recognized that "words can have many meanings" and that as a result constitutional interpretation cannot be simply a matter of looking definitions up in a dictionary. It involves, as well, a rational inquiry into the best understanding and most appropriate means of enforcing the Constitution's guarantees—as he put it, of "seeking to execute policies written into the Constitution."[12] At the same time, while Harlan often stressed that "it is the purposes of those guarantees and not their text" that is the ultimate goal of interpretation, in practice he gave painstaking attention to the language of the Constitution. The long-running dispute between Black and Harlan was a lovers' quarrel that assumed the intelligibility of the Constitution and of the constitutional enterprise; their disagreement was passionate because both were committed to the common endeavor.

Justices Black and Harlan were, then, exemplars of what I am calling the constitutional virtue of faith, and their collegiality in the presence of sharp disagreement was not merely the product of personal sympathy and affection but also a sign of what the virtue of faith enables, the possibility of dialogue. As one of Black's clerks remembered later, Harlan "invariably stop[ped] by to pick Black up going to court and conference and they'd walk down the hall together . . . [while] Black would try with great animation to convince Harlan to go the other way."[13] Faith in the intelligibility of the Constitution makes it possible to discuss issues of its interpretation as problems that we can work together at solving, even if our differing perspectives make it unlikely that we will agree. We can talk together, not just shout at each other. In the absence of faith—belief in and commitment to the intelligible Constitution—constitutional-law talk is merely a form of *argumentum ad baculum*.

We turn now to a second presupposition of the Constitution, one that we saw Attorney General Akerman dealing with in chapter 3: the unavoidable presence of uncertainty in its interpretation and execution. Founding-era constitutionalists understood, correctly I think, that no legal instrument complex in its provisions or in its goals can eliminate ambiguity. This must be true a fortiori for an instrument that it is the constituent act of a nation. The founders therefore accepted quite consciously the corollary that interpreting the Constitution is an intellectually creative activity, not a mechanical process of unveiling outcomes already fixed in the text. Madison was only stating a truism when he wrote in *The Federalist* that "all new laws [including the Constitution], though penned with the greatest technical skill, and passed on the fullest and most mature deliberation, are considered as more or less obscure and equivocal, until their meaning be liquidated and ascertained by a series of particular discussions and adjudications."[14] The Constitution is intelligible, but much of the time its specific meaning, as applied to a specific situation, is not indisputable, at least at first.

From the adoption of the Ninth Amendment on, the Constitution's text has rendered this presupposition explicit: "The enumeration in the Constitution, of certain rights, shall not be construed to deny or disparage others retained by the people." Leave aside the ongoing debate about what use, if any, a court may make of the Ninth Amendment in exercising the power of judicial review; that is a contested question. But what surely cannot be disputed is that the Ninth Amendment acknowledges the possibility of varying constructions of the text: the command not to construe the text in a certain manner implies the rational possibility of doing so. No one has ever felt the need for an amendment disallowing a construction of Article I, Section 8, that invalidates the creation of the Air Force, even though the text enumerates powers only to create an Army and Navy—that interpretation of Article I is absurd. But as the Ninth Amendment shows, the constitutional text admits, again and again, of plausible constructions, many of which must nevertheless be wrong or unacceptable under the supreme law of the excluded middle.

The Ninth Amendment and a few other provisions—the Eleventh Amendment, arguably the enforcement clauses of the Thirteenth and later amendments—are attempts in the text itself to obviate wrongheaded constitutional arguments, but for the most part the Constitution leaves it to its interpreters to deal appropriately with constitutional uncertainty, and after all, even the Ninth Amendment requires interpretation. In the presence of ambiguity, if constitutional interpretation is not to devolve into cynical posturing, interpreters must display the constitutional virtues of integrity and candor: integrity in coming to decision, candor in the presentation of arguments that often can be said to be only the interpreter's best judgment, not the text's unmistakable bidding, on how to enforce the Constitution. Constitutional ambiguity is, as Madison knew, unavoidable, and (as he also knew) uncertainty gives ample room for insincere and manipulative arguments. The virtues of integrity and candor mark the distinction between pretense and reality in constitutional interpretation, and because of that they are indispensable.

No member of the Supreme Court has ever dealt with greater openness about the Constitution's ambiguity than Robert Jackson. Jackson's expression of uncertainty in the *Kahriger* gambling-tax case is well known: he began his concurrence with the statement "I concur in the judgment and opinion of the Court, but with such doubt that if the minority agreed upon an opinion which did not impair legitimate use of the taxing power I probably would join it." *Kahriger* was no sport, moreover: Jackson's opinions on constitutional issues often allude to the necessity of decision in the presence of uncertainty. In a 1941 opinion, for example, he wrote that he did "not ignore or belittle the difficulties" of "giving concrete meaning to [the Constitution's often] obscure and vagrant phrases." "But," he continued, "the difficulty of the task does not excuse us from giving [its] general and abstract words whatever of specific content and concreteness they will bear as we mark out their application."[15]

Justice Jackson's famous concurrence in the Steel Seizure Case is a remarkable exercise in the virtues of integrity and candor. The opinion opens by acknowledging the ambiguities of the Constitution's commands with respect to the powers of the president:

> Just what our forefathers did envision, or would have envisioned had they foreseen modern conditions, must be divined from materials almost as enigmatic as the dreams Joseph was called upon to interpret for Pharaoh. A century and a half of partisan debate and scholarly speculation yields no net result but only supplies more or less apt quotations from respected sources on each side of any question.

At the same time, Jackson admitted, his own experience as an executive-branch lawyer was "probably . . . a more realistic influence on my views" of presidential power "than the conventional materials of judicial decision." What follows is nevertheless a rigorously argued legal analysis of the constitutional issues in the case that many, myself included, think brilliant but that is at the same time a remarkably candid statement of Jackson's assumptions and of the points in the analysis at which Jackson is simply taking a position that is, for him, axiomatic and that others might wish to contest. The opinion's greatness lies not only in Jackson's logic but also in his honesty.

Because of the inescapability of judgment in the interpretation and application of the Constitution, candor is essential if the justices, or whoever is purporting to speak in the voice of the Constitution, are to ask the rest of us to take them seriously where they cannot claim that their judgments are beyond dispute. Only if you and I understand the true grounds of a decision can we assent to its correctness or (and this is the point of greatest moment) to its validity as the outcome of our system even though we think it wrong in substance. Because the Constitution is not a crossword puzzle with only one right answer to its interlocking questions, playing the constitutional-law game fairly demands that the players be clear about why they give the answers they do. Candor is indispensable if the system is to retain its moral dignity; it is candor that all four of our hypothetical justices lack. The constitutional virtue of candor, therefore, goes beyond honesty about the meaning of cases and sincerity in the statement of viewpoint. It is the disposition to seek, and so far as possible to achieve, a congruity between the mind grappling with the constitutional issue before it and the language in which that struggle and its resolution is expressed, "living speech," as James Boyd White has memorably described it.[16]

Candor as a constitutional virtue is inextricably linked with integrity in decision making, the virtue of seeking in any given situation that interpretation of the Constitution that honestly seems to the interpreter the most plausible resolution of the issues in the light of the text and constitutional tradition.[17] Integrity in this sense is not invariably an aspect of legal argument.

This is self-evidently true in litigation, where the adversary process assumes that the parties are advocating views of the law because those views serve the litigants' respective and conflicting
objectives. This perspective is not limited to litigation, moreover. Consider the federal Internal Revenue Code. The taxpayer
is not expected to accept for himself or herself the code's core
purpose, the raising of revenue. Quite to the contrary, she or he
is expected and allowed to attempt to minimize the code's success in fulfilling that purpose and within broad limits can argue
for constructions of the code without making any claim that in
the abstract she believes those interpretations are the best resolution of the code's ambiguities.[18] The code is a tool to which
the taxpayer, at any rate, owes no internal allegiance or, in her
dealings with it, the virtue of integrity.

The same is not true of judges making constitutional decisions—or, I have argued in the previous chapter, of political-
branch lawyers either. (The position of executive-branch lawyers
litigating on behalf of the government may raise some addi-
tional considerations, although I believe that the principle I am
describing basically applies even there.) If Chief Justice Marshall's perspective in *Marbury v. Madison* was right, governmental officials under oath to uphold the Constitution have obliged
themselves, as a matter of personal and institutional morality, to
treat the Constitution not as a tool that they can use to achieve
whatever goals they choose on other grounds, but itself as the
ground for their decisions. The constitutional virtue of integrity
is the ambition and habit of addressing constitutional questions
in this noninstrumentalist fashion and therefore plays no role in
an instrumentalist view of law of the sort that Judge Posner and
others advocate.[19]

Justices John and Johanna possess neither integrity nor candor: they decide constitutional cases on grounds entirely extra-
neous to the words they use in "describing" their votes. Justices
Oliver and Marsha represent more complex stances. I have intended to portray them as wishing to make constitutional decisions with integrity, and chapter 1 argued that the practice of

each makes partial sense. Where they fail is that each, in a different way, is engaged in a sort of self-deception—largely over the truth that the other's position contains. As a consequence, despite their laudable ambitions, their decisions are prone not to engage in a full consideration of all the factors that our constitutional practices treat as relevant, and lacking full candor with themselves, they cannot act with full candor in explaining their decisions. Chapter 3 argued that Attorney General Akerman, in contrast, seems in his civil service opinion to have displayed both integrity and candor: he labored to engage fully with all the issues relevant to the question he was addressing (including what exactly that question was) and to explain his conclusion in such a way that the reader was invited to think the difficult points through with Akerman, and enabled to disagree intelligently if his or her judgment was not the same as Akerman's. Justice Jackson's Steel Seizure opinion is admirable for similar reasons: Jackson's candor in describing how he approached the case convincingly portrays that approach as one of integrity.

↙

Human beings, and especially human beings organized into political societies, typically do not like disagreement. The reasons are perfectly understandable: disagreement on anything above the trivial is confusing, puts harmonious relations at risk, tends to expand and become self-perpetuating, and can spiral into overt and violent conflict. As an historical matter, the typical political response to these dangers has been to try to eliminate their source: if we all agree, the problem disappears. Or that is the implicit theory underlying the long story of social attempts to impose political, ethical, and religious uniformity: we can get rid of disagreement and therefore we should.

The Constitution of the United States starts from exactly the opposite presupposition: disagreement on matters of great importance is ineradicable, and it is a tragic mistake to attempt to eliminate it. The classic founding-era discussion is *The Federal-*

ist, number 10, by Madison: as long as there is liberty, "which is essential to political life," there will be factions, citizens "united and actuated by some common impulse of passion, or of interest" not shared by other citizens, since it is quite impossible to stop different people from coming to different opinions. "The latent causes of faction are . . . sown in the nature of man; and we see them everywhere."[20] Without in the least denying the potentially destructive force of disagreement over political, economic, or religious matters, Madison and other proponents of ratification insisted that the Constitution would deal with such dangers by other means than the attempted imposition of unity in opinion. From the beginning it has been clear that disagreement, even passionate and principled disagreement, with all its regrettable consequences, will always be a feature of political life under the Constitution, because the Constitution embodies a commitment to liberty. In the twenty-first century many of us tend reflexively to think of the First Amendment when we consider the constitutional legitimacy of disagreement, but let us recall that the original Constitution already included an explicit guarantee of disagreement that was bold, even radical against the backdrop of Western history: Article VI's provision that "no religious Test shall ever be required as a Qualification to any Office or public Trust under the United States."[21]

Madison's solution to the problem of faction in *The Federalist* invoked the federal structure of the Republic, but after ratification it quickly became clear that there could be no purely structural answer to the risks disagreement poses to the unity of the community. The Sedition Act of 1798 stands as an early example of the susceptibility of the Constitution's own structural forms to distortion and manipulation by those afraid to run the risk of social conflict. The Constitution's ambition to maintain political community in the midst of radical disagreement can be achieved only if those who act under it possess the constitutional virtue that I shall call humility, the habit of doubting that the Constitution resolves divisive political or social issues as opposed to requiring them to be thrashed out through the processes of ordinary, revisable politics. This is not the same as skepticism or self-doubt: what I mean by the constitutional virtue of humility is perfectly consistent with a strong and even passionate commitment to one's views on contested matters of constitutional interpretation. The virtue manifests itself in a continuing recognition that the Constitution is primarily a framework for political argument and decision and not a tool for the elimination of debate. The result is a humble or limited conception of the role of the Constitution, of the Supreme Court, and of one's own constitutional convictions.[22]

Justice Holmes was not a humble man in any ordinary sense of the adjective, but he consistently displayed the constitutional virtue of humility. Holmes is often understood as a skeptic, of course, but I believe that is inaccurate, at least with reference to his views on constitutional law. Both Holmes's famous deference to political decision making and his post-1918 advocacy of strong constitutional protections for freedom of speech stem from the fact that he understood the Constitution along the lines I have indicated. While Holmes's views on the First Amendment did develop over time, he signaled his basic attitude of humility about the role of the Constitution and the Court at the very beginning of his service on the Supreme Court, in *Otis v. Parker*, decided in 1903. Holmes wrote:

> Considerable latitude must be allowed for differences of view as well as for possible peculiar conditions which this court can know but imperfectly, if at all. Otherwise a constitution, instead of embodying only relatively fundamental rules of right, as generally understood by all English-speaking communities, would become the partisan of a particular set of ethical or economical opinions, which by no means are held semper ubique et ab omnibus.

The existence of honest "differences of view" over the meaning of the Constitution ought to give one pause before concluding that the Constitution forbids the resolution of a social conflict through ordinary politics, that it (in essence) ordains a certain orthodoxy on the matter.[23]

Justice Holmes's famous dissent in *Lochner v. New York* is perhaps the clearest demonstration of the constitutional virtue of humility to be found in the United States Reports. The proposition that Holmes was justifying was his view that the Court majority was in error in holding that a state law regulating the maximum hours bakers might work was an infringement of constitutional liberty. Holmes declined to enter into the debate between the majority and the other dissenting justices about the value of the law, not because he had no views on the matter (that is a misreading of his opinion) but because treating its value as a matter settled by the Constitution was, in his view, to misunderstand the role of the Constitution in American public life: "[A] Constitution is not intended to embody a particular economic theory, whether of paternalism and the organic relation of the citizen to the state or of laissez faire. It is made for people of fundamentally differing views." The Constitution, Holmes perfectly well understood, sometimes does rule out a particular economic, social, or moral theory: our government has no general power to confiscate the entire value of private property regardless of opinions that such a power is moral, desirable, or wise. But as a general matter, the Constitution leaves disagreement in the political realm of conflict and faction, where the big-enders may win today and the little-enders tomorrow, and ensures that the conflict may continue by forbidding governmental attempts to shut down debate.[24]

In *West Virginia State Board of Education v. Barnette*, the Supreme Court held, in the midst of World War II, that a mandatory school flag salute was unconstitutional. Speaking through Justice Jackson the Court asserted, "If there is any fixed star in our constitutional constellation, it is that no official, high or petty, can prescribe what shall be orthodox in politics, nationalism, religion, or other matters of opinion or force citizens to confess by word or act their faith therein." The constitutional virtue of humility is a predisposition to recall not only that legislators and executive officers may not prescribe an orthodoxy through law, but that the Constitution itself is such an orthodoxy only in a narrow and limited sense, that our presumption ought to be that political and social disagreement is addressed in the contingent and revisable forms of politics.[25]

Humility in the sense I am using the term is easily confused with a substantive jurisprudence of judicial deference to the political process. *Barnette* itself, as we just noted, invalidated a statute that was the product of democratic electoral practices and legislative decision; Justice Frankfurter, who strongly believed in a very high degree of deference to legislatures, dissented on strongly put democratic grounds. The virtue of humility is the habit in constitutional decision making to resist the natural tendency of societies and individuals to avoid conflict, either by judicial decisions that remove debatable issues from the political sphere altogether or by political actions that curtail the public expression of divergent or dissenting views. A justice or other official can display humility in reaching a constitutional judgment contrary to the politically ordained outcome (as I believe the justices did in *Barnette*), and by the same token a substantively deferential constitutional decision can fail to respect and maintain the Constitution's openness to faction and conflict.

↚

In *Missouri v. Holland*, of which we have already taken note, Justice Holmes found it necessary in addressing a particular constitutional question to describe the constitutional project that makes us the community we are. Sometimes the answer to a constitutional question can be found only by considering what the aim of the whole enterprise is, what goals can be ascribed to constitutional law, what sense we can make of the Republic not just as a posited reality, capable of doing harm to people who become crosswise with its force, but also as an enterprise that is meant to do good to people along lines that have been laid out in advance. The Constitution presupposes, in other words, that not only its words but also its purposes are comprehensible and humanly attractive. Since it is quite clearly possible for intelligent human beings to disagree radically over those purposes—Abraham Lincoln and Jefferson Davis were not distinguishable in either their sincerity or their intelligence—this fact about the constitutional system implies that there must be some way of dealing with radical, turtles-all-the-way-down disagreement over how we are to understand the goals of the constitutional enterprise.

One solution, a comfortable one for many lawyers because of its familiarity, is to give dispositive weight to past constitutional decisions. Stare decisis—Stand by the decision!—is an age-old principle of the common law and lies at the heart of American legal reasoning, including reasoning about the Constitution. As president, James Madison signed into law a bill creating a national bank even though a quarter century earlier he had vigorously assailed a constitutionally indistinguishable bill as an invalid usurpation of power. Madison, however, firmly rejected the charge of inconsistency: Madison's personal judgment that the best reading of Article I—that it does not authorize a national bank—might be unchanged, but the nation had decided differently, through repeated actions by all three branches of the federal government. In such a circumstance, the individual interpreter is obliged to submit his judgment to the contrary one adopted by the Republic's institutions:

> Has the wisest and most conscientious judge ever scrupled to acquiesce in decisions in which he has been overruled by the matured opinions of the majority of his colleagues, and subsequently to conform himself thereto, as to authoritative expositions of the law? . . . That there may be extraordinary and peculiar circumstances controlling the rule . . . may be admitted, but with such exceptions the rule will force itself on the practical judgment

of the most ardent theorist. He will find it impossible to adhere, and act officially upon, his solitary opinions as to the meaning of the law or Constitution, in opposition to a construction reduced to practice during a reasonable period of time.[26]

In the case of the bank, Madison believed that Congress's repeated conclusion after full debate that it possessed the power at issue, President Washington's considered decision to sign the first bank bill into law, and the judicial decisions enforcing the provisions of that law were too sustained a "course of precedents" to permit him to ignore "all the obligations" such a course of practice created. His duty "as a public man," was to act in accordance with the precedent rather than "to sacrifice all these public considerations to my private opinion."

Madison did not intend this view of precedent, furthermore, to be a merely prudential consideration; it was, he wrote, the "constitutional rule of interpreting a Constitution." Precisely because constitutional law involves the interpretation of words that also are a constituent act, their interpretation is a public affair in which the interpreter, at least when acting officially, cannot properly reach decisions solely on the basis of his or her personal, solitary opinions.[27]

Can we then solve the problem of how to deal with principled disagreement by the doctrine of stare decisis, expanded perhaps to include political as well as judicial precedent? (But then what of conflict between them?) Even if this might be a comfortable solution for some lawyers, it is not a tenable one if taken too literally. The reader will have noted that Madison himself put certain qualifications on his "constitutional rule" of abiding by constitutional decisions: to be binding on the conscientious decision maker, a particular "construction" of the Constitution must have been "reduced to practice during a reasonable period of time"—the first law enacted or case decided on a controversial issue does not at once exclude further debate or reconsideration (it is the "matured opinions" of the judge's colleagues that bind), and even a settled interpretation might not be obligatory in some ("extraordinary and peculiar") circumstances. Even more important, as Madison's own reasoning suggests, our practices include a long-standing, rich tradition of constitutional second thoughts. Many of the building blocks of modern constitutional law—on the scope of Congress's powers, the requirements of the First Amendment, the meaning of equality—are the product of both the Court and the political branches reconsidering and ultimately rejecting past decisions. There is no absolute rule of constitutional stare decisis, and our constitutional law would be humanly unattractive if there were.

However, as we saw in our earlier consideration of humility and judicial deference, where there is no rule, there may be room for the exercise of a constitutional virtue. Let us adopt Madison's term and call it the virtue of acquiescence, the predisposition to accept the premises of existing decisions even when they are not our own premises, to accept that a question can be settled and ought to be taken as a starting point for further constitutional thought, not as an opportunity for endless reargument. This makes no sense, of course, to those like Justices John and Johanna who see constitutional law in a purely instrumental light—for them what one says about past decisions is as irrelevant to their actual choices as any other aspect of law except as a matter of prudence. Justice Oliver accepts stare decisis, of course, as one of the legitimate tools of legal analysis, but his insistence on the sheer apolitical-ness of constitutional law cramps his understanding of precedent, which can too easily become for him an "authority" to be followed (or distinguished or overruled) rather than a guide to thought. Justice Marsha's implicit privileging of her own vision of what is the best constitutional outcome also undermines her understanding of the role of past decisions: she is likely to miss the questions they ought to raise about her own certainties.

The virtue of acquiescence in our tradition of judicial and political precedent is crucial to the constitutional conscience, but as I have suggested, it is the exercise of a moral obligation rather than obedience to an invariant rule of decision. Whether in any given situation a constitutional interpreter on or off the Court ought to acquiesce in a decision that in his or her "solitary" opinion is wrong cannot be determined abstractly. Such a judgment must be particular to the issue at hand. In habitually beginning from a presumption of respect for past decisions, the conscientious interpreter acknowledges the possibility not only of error on his or her part, but even more fundamentally the existence of principled disagreement within the American community over the Constitution's purposes. The virtue of acquiescence locates the constitutional decision maker within the broader American community, which encompasses the past, with its controversies, conclusions, and errors, as well as his or her contemporaries, who share that past, as well as the obligation to treat constitutional decision as the search to implement not a partisan or parochial perspective but what Madison called "the national judgment and intention."

I have identified what I believe are certain constitutional virtues, dispositions of mind and will that are necessary if men and women are to interpret and apply the Constitution as that instrument and the history of our dealings with it demand. Without those virtues as ideals, and as realities, to the extent that is possible for fallible human beings, American constitutionalism is a fraud. In itself, this observation tells us nothing about the significance of the constitutional virtues outside the specific context of trying to play the constitutional-law game fairly. The disposition or habit of following the card play closely is a virtue in playing the game of bridge, but of no obvious or immediate importance outside that context. You should cultivate it if you like to play bridge, but there is no moral obligation to like or play the game. Constitutional law, in contrast, is quite different: there is, within the American political system, no way not to play, even if in no other sense than that of being subject to the constitutional decisions of the Court and other governmental actors, and a great deal of what constitutional law addresses—think of war or abortion or the way we treat those we accuse of crimes—is unmistakably laden with moral significance that goes beyond the game. And here we see how the constitutional virtues serve to give moral content to constitutional law. The constitutional virtues of faith, integrity, candor, humility, and acquiescence are essential to the game, but their moral significance is not limited to that game: they draw the outline of a particular attitude toward political community. Confidence in the possibility of dialogue, recognition of the inescapability of judgment, humility in the imposition of one's own opinions, acquiescence in decisions that seem wrong to one's own judgment but have persuaded others—these are not just a habit like following the cards, they describe the characteristics of men and women who recognize the incorrigible otherness of those with whom they must live and yet who decline the old, sour, ultimately violent solution of denying the equal humanity of the other.

Justice Holmes once wrote that he objected to the "attitude of absoluteness" he detected in Henry James's fiction because it "exclud[ed] from the heights all those who do not share [James's] scale of values." Holmes's criticism did not rest on the relativism often (if wrongly) ascribed to him: Holmes was quite willing to pass private judgment on the views of those he thought ignorant or wrongheaded. He thought such judgments, however, necessarily private. In the public realm of the American political community, we must act on the assumption that what fundamentally unites us is not agreement—or coercion—but a willingness to listen to the other even when we disagree strongly and on grounds of high principle. "There is enough community for us to talk, not enough for anyone to command."[28] Of course, this formulation is not to be taken literally: government, including the judiciary's enforcement of the Constitution, rests on society's recognition of its legitimate authority to command. In the absence of such recognition, the state would have only brute force on which to rely. Holmes's point is that the unavoidably coercive aspect of political community is, in the American system, dependent on conversation, on the ability of those subject to its coercions to participate in the community's choices. The constitutional virtues collectively inculcate a predisposition to understand American constitutionalism in this manner, as a privileging of talk over command, inclusive conversation over divisive exercises of power. Where the virtues hold sway, American political community will be resistant to the temptations to prejudice, cruelty, and heartlessness that are omnipresent in the human condition.

To interpret and apply this Constitution, Americans must embody the constitutional virtues; to be a humane and decent society we must do the same. Men and women of goodwill need not reject involvement in constitutional law as a condition of their claim to goodwill and civility. The practice of constitutional decision making, engaged in fairly and according to the rules, is itself a training in civility.

5 ← Making It Up as We Go Along

In *James B. Beam Distilling Co. v. Georgia*, the Supreme Court rejected the propriety of employing "selective prospectivity" in civil litigation: when in a civil case the Court announces a new rule of law and applies the new rule in that case, the Court concluded that the judiciary is obliged to apply the new rule to the parties in other pending civil actions as well.[1] Justice Antonin Scalia explained that in his view the employment of selective prospectivity amounts to an unconstitutional judicial exercise of the power to make law. He then continued in a rather curious vein.

> I am not so naive (nor do I think our forebears were) as to be unaware that judges in a real sense "make" law. But they make it *as judges make it*, which is to say *as though* they were "finding" it—discerning what the law *is*, rather than decreeing what it is today *changed to*, or what it will *tomorrow* be.[2]

Justice Byron R. White was not amused. While he agreed with the decision to abandon selective prospectivity in civil cases, he saw no merit in Scalia's distinction: since judges in a real sense do make law, White thought it bizarre, perhaps even offensive, to pretend otherwise, and Scalia's remarks amounted to the suggestion that "judges (in an unreal sense, I suppose) should never concede that they do [make law] and must claim that they do no more than discover it, hence suggesting that there are citizens who are naive enough to believe them. . . . I am quite unpersuaded by this line of reasoning." As Justice Sandra Day O'Connor put it, "Of course, we 'make' law as we go along."[3]

What Justice Scalia meant is not clear—he did not respond to Justice White's sardonic comment—but White's point is vitally important in any event. Exercising the constitutional virtue of candor demands that justices, and other constitutional decision makers in their own spheres, acknowledge that constitutional law is necessarily a creative endeavor. A constitutional-law decision on a significant and debatable matter is not, and cannot be, an analogue to the solution of a crossword puzzle, or the answer to a problem in geometry. *Any* answer to such a question can only be accompanied, if the decision maker is honest, with the recognition that the answer proffered must be uncertain, subject to dispute, an exercise of humility in the constitutional-virtue sense because the decision maker must come to a conclusion and therefore select between discordant but defensible outcomes. (Think of Attorney General Akerman.) Justices, and other constitutional decision makers, come to their constitutional decisions by reasoning that is neither algorithmic nor incontestable.

Although Supreme Court opinions do not always acknowledge this truth about the justices' decisions, Justice White's comment in *Beam* is entirely apposite. Unless the justices (and other constitutional decision makers) are to be indifferent to the moral circumstances in which they decide, they must make constitutional decisions with an open recognition that they are engaged in what is at times a creative enterprise of making law. As Judge Robert Bork correctly observed, in a case involving the application of the First Amendment:

> Judges generalize, they articulate concepts, they enunciate such things as four-factor frameworks, three-pronged tests, and two-tiered analyses in an effort, laudable by and large, to bring order to a universe of unruly happenings and to give guidance for the future to themselves and to others. But it is certain that life will bring up cases whose facts simply cannot be handled by purely verbal formulas, or at least not handled with any sophistication and feel-

ing for the underlying values at stake. When such a case
appears and a court attempts nevertheless to force the old
construct upon the new situation, the result is mechanical jurisprudence. Here we face such a case, and it seems
to me better to revert to first principles than to employ
categories which, in these circumstances, inadequately
enforce the first amendment's design.[4]

In this opinion Judge Bork made two assertions that are, I believe, beyond dispute.

One is the simple observation that a great deal of constitutional law is undeniably the creation of the judges who articu-
late it, as opposed to the logical outworking of anything that
can be ascribed to the indisputable meaning of the constitutional text. The judiciary, the justices of the Supreme Court
centrally, necessarily make novel constitutional law in the effort to give life to the commands of the historical Constitution:
Justice Jackson once wrote, "Only those heedless of legal history can deny that in construing the Constitution the Supreme
Court from time to time makes new constitutional law or alters
the law that has been. And it is idle to say that this is merely the
ordinary process of interpretation."[5] In interpreting and applying the constituent act that the Constitution embodies, the
justices are unavoidably creators of constitutional law that they
have made up. The connection between this form of constitutional law and the Constitution as a document is rhetorical, although not in the invidious sense the adjective often conveys.
The proper question a reader can ask, the demand that she is
entitled to press on the justice or other decision maker, concerns the persuasiveness of the argument presented as a way
of talking about the enterprise that the document constitutes.
Criticisms of Supreme Court opinions that boil down to the
charge that the Court's reasoning cannot be read off the face of
the constitutional text are usually true and invariably beside the
point. The same can be said about constitutional law going all
the way back to *Marbury v. Madison* and *M'Culloch v. Maryland*.

There is no possibility of return to a noncreative form of constitutional decision making, because that is not and has never been an option.

The other point, reflecting Judge Bork's recognition that the Constitution demands faith in its intelligibility, is that judges (and other decision makers) can revert to first principles in a principled manner even when those principles are in dispute. (Judge Bork was in express disagreement in the case with then-Judge Scalia over the principles embodied in the First Amendment.) When Bork wrote that "[w]e are required, therefore, to continue the evolution of the law in accordance with the deepest rationale of the first amendment,"[6] he necessarily assumed that one can discuss the deepest rationale of a constitutional provision even with someone—Judge Scalia, in this case—who doesn't start off, and may not end up, in agreement over that rationale. American constitutional law does not escape, or obviate, the sharpest possible disagreement over its principles. Bork knew that Scalia, a constitutional lawyer of equal ability, disagreed on those principles, and yet Bork—correctly—thought it possible to engage in a conversation over the deepest rationale of the First Amendment.

Judge Bork encapsulated what animates the virtue of faith in ongoing constitutional conversation in his metaphor of evolution in constitutional law. Constitutional law changes, and yet it remains anchored in the text agreed on as supreme law and in the ongoing stream of interpretations of the text, political as well as judicial, that make up constitutional law.[7] Constitutional decision makers unavoidably—and rightly—address constitutional problems by asking what the most sensible resolution to the problem is in light of "the project which makes us the community we are" in the here and now.[8] At the same time, our constitutional practices make it clear that the decision maker is responsible not just to the felt needs of the day but to the ongoing project or enterprise of American political community, an enterprise of which he or she is the interpreter rather than the creator. Constitutional decisions, conscientiously reached, will

sometimes be novel or surprising if viewed from the perspective of the past, but that is only to say that constitutional law is
a tradition that evolves, and that what gives it moral continuity
resides in great measure in a shared sense of responsibility on
the part of those who make the decisions.

A conscientious justice (or other interpreter) will reach decisions and write opinions within a framework shaped by the
virtues that enact this responsibility: humility about the role of
the Court and other institutions as servants, not masters, of the
constitutional system; acquiescence in past interpretations and
decisions; integrity in reaching his or her judgment about how
to address the issue at hand in the light of both the past and
the present; candor so that the reader can follow and if need be
reject the interpreter's reasoning. Our practices richly confirm
Chief Justice Marshall's insistence in *Marbury v. Madison* that
constitutional decision is an ethical activity, one that demands
individual moral choices by the interpreter—integrity in constitutional judgment is integrity in resolving interpretive difficulties in the way most persuasive to the interpreter him or herself,
however much the virtue of acquiescence properly structures
what is persuasive. As Attorney General Akerman's opinion on
the civil service commission illustrates, constitutional-law reasoning in a difficult case is a matter not of offering logical proofs, but
of making contestable judgments, judgments that may involve
weighing a balance, drawing a line, judging a question of degree,
that cannot be reduced to legal algebra. There is no escape, not
even in theory, from the problem of how to play the game fairly,
no set of determinate, substantive principles that are somehow
the unwritten meaning of the Constitution, adherence to which
validates one's choices in constitutional decision making. There
is no escape, not even for legal instrumentalists such as Judge Posner, from individual moral responsibility in constitutional law.

Much rides, then, on the consciences of the justices and others
called upon to reach decisions about the Constitution's operative
meaning. But fortunately, this is not a counsel of moral perfectionism, as if in the end men needed to be angels to make American

constitutionalism a going concern. The virtues implicit in the Constitution's presuppositions and the conscience necessary to our practices are aspects of the decision makers' public personae as officials of the Republic. It is possible, up to a point, both to inculcate them and to gauge their presence—or absence—in the work of those who make constitutional decisions. Constitutional law is a system of words, a language, as well as a system for the application of power, and it is through the public character of that language that we can both cultivate and critique constitutional decision. The paradigmatic expression of constitutional language is the Supreme Court opinion—the core of education in constitutional law as well as the central model for the constitutional statements written by other officials and lawyers. Others have cataloged the defects of the contemporary opinion-writing practices of the Court (ghostwriting by clerks, elephantine length, the prevalence of cutting and pasting and the string citation, incivility), and I shall not repeat their work here.[9] What is important to say in this book is that there is no insurmountable difficulty in correcting whatever problems there are.

One crucial need, as the late Professor Joseph Goldstein wrote in a wise little book several years ago, is for the justices' opinions to make clear sense as exercises in persuasive writing rather than to hide behind a brittle and lifeless facade invigorated only by angry polemic.[10] In cases involving difficult constitutional issues—and the Supreme Court decides few constitutional cases that do not—the burden is on the opinion writer, where writing for the Court or separately, to persuade the reader. Everyone, I assume, agrees that opinions that rest on faulty logic or unconvincing readings of text, structure, and precedent do not persuade: their force is entirely institutional and authoritarian, and even those happy with the outcome should be dissatisfied with the process. But the Constitution does not belong to the justices, and while our practices include respect for the rulings of the Court regardless of their persuasiveness, that respect presumes a corollary respect for the rest of us on the part of the Court. The Court plays its part in the system only when its members make it clear through their words that they are genuinely engaged with the hard issues before them, and that they are being honest with themselves and with us about the considerations that drive them. Only when their opinions seek to persuade our judgments, not just coerce our wills, can the decisions of the Court truly be called authoritative.[11]

The viability, both socially and morally, of our constitutional practices thus depends vitally on the Court—but does anyone doubt this regardless of his or her view of practices or Court? The justices themselves, of course, ultimately must respond to this demand,[12] but there is much that the rest of us can do as well. If the account I have given of our practices is accurate, the teaching of constitutional law ought to have more to do with how constitutional questions can be resolved with integrity and their resolution expressed with clarity—which would entail greater focus on the justices' opinions as expository writing rather than announcements of position (and teaching materials designed for that purpose). Lower-court judges can ignore whatever bad examples of excessive detail, slipshod reasoning, and bad manners the justices insist on providing. Congress and the press can urge the executive branch to make public a greater percentage of the opinions written by the executive's lawyers, and the executive and the press can spotlight Congress's failures to address on its own serious constitutional problems in proposed legislation. None of this is difficult, none of it is even very dramatic, but it is only through such means that the Court's own behavior will change. For one of the moral circumstances in which the justices make constitutional decisions is the contemporary tendency to condone a system in which the justices no longer do their own work, as Justice Louis Brandeis once boasted they did,[13] and generally allow it to be done poorly. Like the instrumental view of the strong Rule of Five, this is a moral circumstance that the justices can and ought to resist, and the starting point for resistance is to name the problem.

The continuity over time of American constitutionalism, like the coherence of its practices at any given moment, rests in large measure in the ethical structure of constitutional law, the exercise by the decision makers of the constitutional virtues. I do not believe it follows, however, that both continuity and coherence reside entirely in a conscientious process of decision making.[14] While it is true that American constitutional law is a game played by fair observance of the rules, not by the discovery of the right answers in the way that one does a crossword puzzle, there is a bit more that one can say about the answers that fair play allows. A conscientious desire to make constitutional decisions fairly will push the decision maker in certain directions, even if conscience does not predetermine the outcomes in (most?) particular cases. The justices make up constitutional law, but the law they make up is not a free-form composition. There is a substantive, if quite broad, relationship between the virtues that the Constitution implicitly demands of its interpreters and the substance of its commands as they will appear to any conscientious interpreter in the early twenty-first century. So, then, what substantive commitments correlate with the constitutional virtues that condition the process of constitutional decision making?

THE PRIORITY OF THE POLITICAL. I might equally have referred to the priority of democracy, except that the latter term often brings with it romantic notions about "the will" of "the people." American constitutionalism implies nothing of the sort. It is, instead, resolutely antiromantic. In the American Republic the political process is not some means of channeling the choices (which if they existed would be authoritarian and frightening) of a mythical people: it is instead the form of political struggle by which individuals and groups seek to pursue their own goals within a shared political framework. In Learned Hand's words, American "democracy [is] a political contrivance by which the group conflicts inevitable in all society should find a relatively harmless outlet in the give and take of legislative compromise after the contending groups ha[ve] a chance to measure their relative strengths."[15] At our best, as individuals and groups we take into account the existence of fellow Americans with (sometimes) very different visions of the world, but the Constitution does not assume that we are always at our best, nor does it demand that we be so. Instead, it gives priority to a political system in which public policy is, for the most part, reversible because it is a product of electoral politics. As a general matter, therefore—and this is the core meaning not only of the New Deal constitutional revolution but of the Marshall Court's decision in *M'Culloch v. Maryland* as well—the Constitution permits transient majorities to do what they will, all in the expectation that so long as the political process is not frozen, a new majority will sweep away policies that have come to seem regrettable to enough voters. The importance of the constitutional virtue of humility is the check it places on the temptation to treat as constitutionally ordained—and thus beyond the scope of politics—issues that fairly lie within this broad political realm.

THE ABSENCE OF ORTHODOXY. It is a commonplace that the Constitution does not allow government to restrict or prohibit freedom of thought or, except in narrow circumstances, freedom of speech and expression. The underlying rationale is, however, not always recognized. American constitutionalism is a political system that empowers our governmental institutions to take action about what those in authority think must be done, but that does not require anyone, holding any views, to agree with the decision of the majority. We have already encountered the canonical statement of this principle, written by Justice Robert Jackson in *West Virginia State Board of Education v. Barnette.* The issue was the constitutionality of a state law requiring public school students to salute the United States flag; the Court struck down the law as a violation of constitutional free speech. Justice Jackson wrote for the Court,

> If there is any fixed star in our constitutional constellation, it is that no official, high or petty, can prescribe what shall be orthodox in politics, nationalism, religion,

or other matters of opinion or force citizens to confess by word or act their faith therein. If there are any circumstances which permit an exception, they do not now occur to us.

The principle, if we are to take it seriously, cannot be only a rule limiting governmental interference with free expression. It is equally a rule of political morality. No one in this system is obliged to accept as true or right the ethical content of an American political decision, including a decision by the Supreme Court about the meaning and application of the Constitution.

This is a hard rule. All of us have views that we do not see as negotiable. Those who disagree with us about them we believe to be simply wrong, and wrong in a fundamental sense. It is natural to want to treat someone so wrong as in some sense an alien, outside our own political community. But American constitutionalism takes a different tack: "[I]f there is any principle of the Constitution that more imperatively calls for attachment than any other it is the principle of free thought—not free thought for those who agree with us but freedom for the thought that we hate."[16] The Constitution establishes a system through which disputes can be resolved, and it authorizes the use of force to require that the resolutions it generates be obeyed. But it does not require anyone to agree that these resolutions are morally or even constitutionally right in principle. The conscience of every American remains free. Constitutional decisions reflecting integrity and candor on the part of the interpreter will recognize the legitimacy of disagreement.

THE INCLUSION OF EVERYONE. The original constitutional text left it unclear who was a member of the body politic. The most distinguished antebellum attorney general, William Wirt, concluded that defining citizenship was resigned to the states, and Chief Justice Roger Brooke Taney went a step further and ruled that the Constitution itself denied citizenship to African Americans. In contrast, a prominent proslavery judge, Edwin Ruffin, insisted that black Americans were part of "our people," while Attorney General Edward Bates directly contradicted Chief Justice Taney and concluded that race played no role in defining membership in the American body politic.[17] The Fourteenth Amendment resolved the argument between Bates and Taney—"All persons born or naturalized in the United States, and subject to the jurisdiction thereof, are citizens of the United States"—and extended the law's domain even beyond that broad definition: the states are forbidden to injure "any person" without due process or deny her "the equal protection of the laws." The community of those who count, whose voices must be heard, is effectively coterminous with the limits of American authority.

The full implications of this principle remain unclear. The Fourteenth Amendment has given rise to a judicially enforceable rule, which is for the most part noncontroversial, that public actions which exclude individuals or groups from full membership in the community on religious, ethnic or racial grounds are unconstitutional. The extent to which the principle imposes an affirmative duty on those who wield political power to ensure the full inclusion of everyone is debatable and there is ongoing disagreement over the application of the principle to unlawful immigrants and gay and lesbian people, among other groups. This should not surprise us, nor does it render the principle meaningless. The existence of continuing debate bears on whether a decision maker ought to acquiesce in a decision he or she believes erroneous, but it is also a sign of the continuing vitality of the constitutional tradition.

←

Justice White was right: the members of the Supreme Court—and other constitutional interpreters—do not simply discover the law of the Constitution. No legal craft (think of Justice Oliver), constitutional perfectionism (Justice Marsha of course), or theory of interpretation or judicial review (not even Professor Ely's great book) can obviate the need at times for the most conscientious decision maker to make choices among plausible interpretations of the Constitution. Our constitutional practices nevertheless assume, in both the language we use and the authority we grant them, that constitutional decisions can be made through a principled evaluation of constitutional arguments—and not on the basis of the will, the preferences or the extraconstitutional values of the decision makers. Those practices can only make sense, therefore, if such a mode of principled constitutional decision is possible. The only possible locus for such a mode of decision lies in the constitutional conscience of the decision maker, a conscience shaped by the virtues that correspond to the basic presuppositions of the Constitution.

If this is true, as I take it to be, thinking about our constitutional system might well produce a vertiginous feeling, as if we were peering over the abyss into a political void. Rather than resting securely in some domain of conclusions beyond human interference—clear textual meaning, original intention, self-evident moral truth, economic efficiency—the fundamental law of the Republic is the scene of human disputation and decision. If Alasdair MacIntyre's account of contemporary society's moral condition—that it is a wasteland of incommensurable moral assertions—is accurate, this truly would be frightening. American constitutionalism is a gamble that American society is not MacIntyre's wasteland. Let us turn one last time to Justice Holmes for what is perhaps the most famous statement of that wager.

In his seminal 1919 dissent in *Abrams v. United States*, a case interpreting the scope of the free speech clause of the First Amendment, Holmes made what is on the face of it a surprising concession to totalitarian government: "Persecution for the expression of opinions seems to me perfectly logical. If you have no doubt of your premises or your power and want a certain result with all your heart you naturally express your wishes in law and sweep away all opposition." Given Holmes's strong commitment to majoritarian government—recall that he endorsed the constitutional legitimacy of "the natural outcome of a dominant opinion" expressed in law—it would not have been illogical to expect him to follow with a narrow reading of the free expression guaranteed by the First Amendment. Instead, however, Holmes proposed a very different approach to the evaluation of restrictions on speech that the dominant opinion in society favors:

> [W]hen men have realized that time has upset many fighting faiths, they may come to believe even more than they believe the very foundations of their own conduct that the ultimate good desired is better reached by free trade in ideas—that the best test of truth is the power of the thought to get itself accepted in the competition of the market, and that truth is the only ground upon which their wishes safely can be carried out. That at any rate is the theory of our Constitution. It is an experiment, as all life is an experiment. Every year if not every day we have to wager our salvation upon some prophecy based upon imperfect knowledge. While that experiment is part of our system I think that we should be eternally vigilant against attempts to check the expression of opinions that we loathe and believe to be fraught with death, un-less they so imminently threaten immediate interference with the lawful and pressing purposes of the law that an immediate check is required to save the country.[18]

Put another way, Holmes saw the American Constitution as a moral choice to play out a profound freedom in the public square, one that allows the individual to speak in ways that the rest of us fear profoundly, in the hope that doing so will serve a value—truth in this instance—that we all can share.

If the argument of this little book is correct, Holmes's wager is one that American constitutionalism makes not just about the First Amendment and free speech, but about the enterprise of constitutional law as a whole. There is no way to avoid the temp-tation that the Rule of Five presents, no means of playing the game fairly and according to the rules, no theory that eliminates the uncertainty of decisions that are questions of degree, no method that prevents the enterprise of making it up as we go along into one of making up whatever the decision maker prefers—except to play the game as men and women of civility acting in good faith. We are, in the end, thrown back on our moral resources as citizens and as a society. Our constitutional practices assume that those resources will be sufficient. There is no guarantee that they will be.

CONCLUSION ❖ To Govern Ourselves in a Certain Manner

The Supreme Court's first great constitutional decision, *Chisholm v. Georgia*, was also its first great public relations disaster. *Chisholm* held that Article III authorized the Court to exercise jurisdiction over a state at the suit of a citizen of another state; within two years of the decision, the cumbersome amendment process of Article V had overturned the decision through what we now refer to as the Eleventh Amendment.[1] The nation's swift rejection of the decision was doubtless one of many reasons that Chief Justice John Jay, who was in the majority in *Chisholm* but resigned from the Court in 1795 to become governor of New York, declined reappointment in 1801. As Jay informed President John Adams, he "left the bench perfectly convinced" that the Court would never "obtain the energy, weight, and dignity which are essential to its affording due support to the national government, nor acquire the public confidence and respect which, as the last resort of the justice of the nation, it should possess."[2] Jay's unhappiness with his experience on the Court is understandable—in addition to the negative popular reaction to *Chisholm*, the physical burdens of a justice's duties (which included hundreds of miles of travel on circuit each year) were wearying—but it is difficult to imagine any twenty-first-century nominee declining appointment on Jay's ground that the Court lacks energy, weight, dignity, or public confidence and respect. The Court's history has not been without its low points, but in the present it clearly enjoys the central role in national government and in our constitutional system that Jay thought it never would. The fact that Congress and the states have used Article V only three other times since the 1790s to reverse judicial decisions is emblematic of Jay's failure as a prophet, and of the Court's institutional success.[3] The problem with our constitutional system, some argue, is that the Court has been too successful and that as a result the people's Constitution has been monopolized by a Court that is meant to be their as well as its servant.

In his first inaugural, Abraham Lincoln (with the infamous Dred Scott decision in view) counseled against allowing "the policy of the government, upon vital questions, affecting the whole people, . . . to be irrevocably fixed by decisions of the Supreme Court"; if the nation allows that, "the people will have ceased to be their own rulers, having, to that extent, practically resigned their government, into the hands of that eminent tribunal." Across American history, Lincoln's warning has frequently been echoed by critics of particular lines of decision, and a growing body of recent scholarship argues more generally that the Constitution ought to be "taken back" by the people from an arrogant judiciary that has long overstepped its proper bounds.[4] There is, from the perspective I have outlined in this book, considerable truth in Lincoln's concern. The difference between constitutional interpretation and political policy is less clearly defined than someone like Justice Oliver assumes, and the capabilities and temptations of Article III judges are not categorically different from those of interpreters in nonjudicial settings: why, then, should the Court monopolize interpretation? And when the Court does address constitutional issues, I have argued that at the heart of a faithful justice's conscience, shaping his or her view of what the Court should decide, are constitutional virtues of humility and acquiescence that counsel against judicial arrogance and overconfidence. The Constitution's fundamental acceptance of the inevitability of principled conflict and disagreement over not only the policies of the day but also the very purposes of the American project is not a license to argue granted to a professional elite. It is a social commitment, by an ongoing and inclusive political community, that both project and community belong to the whole.

Chief Justice Jay's opinion in the ill-fated *Chisholm* case rested his interpretation of Article III on this understanding of the Constitution. "The attention and attachment of the Constitution to the equal rights of the people are discernable [*sic*] in almost every sentence." The people, not as a mystical corporate body but as a community of individuals, "are truly the sovereigns of the country, but they are sovereigns without subjects,"⁵ "perfectly equal" in their status as members of the community. The "popular sovereignty" that established the Constitution and from which it derives its legitimate authority is one in which "every citizen partakes." The words of Article III ought to be given their natural meaning and states are suable by citizens of other states in federal court precisely because as a constitutional matter the institutions of government are the servants, not the masters, of the people.⁶ However unhappy Jay may have been with the country's quick repudiation of the Court's decision, the process by which that was done was a striking vindication in practice of the account of popular sovereignty Jay had given in *Chisholm*.

The Court, then, does not own the Constitution, but it does not follow that the answers to questions about its interpretation ought to be decided by referendum (and still less by opinion poll). As Jay wrote, the Constitution "is a compact by the people of the United States to govern themselves as to general objects, in a certain manner," and as the supremacy clause of Article VI makes clear, the Constitution is a commitment to be governed under and through "law." Under our practices, by an understanding dating back to the first years of the Republic, this means that questions of constitutional meaning are questions of law, to be resolved through the forms of legal argument. As we have seen, the constitutional virtues are necessary to make this possible in the face of the Constitution's ambiguities and the inevitable presence of questions of degree in difficult cases. Any morally responsible involvement in the constitutional enterprise thus demands the constitutional virtue of faith as I have described it: confidence that it is possible to make sense of what we must do to interpret the Constitution as law, and a commitment to do what is required. In addition, and critically, the virtues bring the decisions of the justices and other officials within the scope of informed criticism by the political community at large. We govern ourselves "in a certain manner" that includes privileging constitutional *law* while expecting those who declare (and sometimes make up) what the law is to act with consciences informed by their role as what Jay called "the agents of the people." The Supreme Court's centrality in practice in the system that has evolved to do this and the justification for placing issues of judicial review at the heart of the inquiry I have undertaken lie not in the primacy of the Court per se, but in the primacy of law.

Chief Justice Jay believed that the Constitution embodies, for this specific political community, "the promise which every free government makes to every free citizen, of equal justice and protection." Our constitutional practices, and the conscience and virtues they demand and require, are our ongoing effort to redeem that promise. By their oaths, as Chief Justice Marshall suggested long ago, the justices and other public officials obligate themselves, as responsible and moral individuals, to that project. By its own internal logic, its rejection of any ideological or philosophical orthodoxy, the Constitution does not enforce the same sort of obligation on those of us who have taken no oath. Its demand on them, on us, is really an invitation to live out in the political and moral life of the Republic at large the virtues which the Constitution expects of its official interpreters. The constitutional project is incomplete, indeed it is at risk, if those virtues, or their political analogues, are limited to those under oath. The life of the citizen, too, involves moral choice and moral responsibility.

There are a great many objections that a reasonable person can make to American constitutionalism. Leave aside the painful charge that we have been insincere and hypocritical in living out our ideals—an accusation that I believe we must accept on many counts: the discrepancy between Chief Justice Jay's language and the slaveholding practices of his era will have escaped no one, and in the future others may say the same about our words and deeds. The ideals themselves can be accused of fantasy, a failure to see that the political enjoys priority in a much harsher sense than I have conceded, that there is not and cannot be anything other than the agonistic struggle of political preferences. These critiques, implicit and explicit, may well be right, or more precisely they may turn out to be true of the United States in the long retrospective of history. Constitutional law is an experiment, as all life is an experiment. The experiment is modest in its goals—we have not formed a political community to bring about the Kingdom of God or even the classless society. Our goals have been to alleviate human suffering and to empower men and women to live their lives as they see fit but to do so in a political community that demands their allegiance to it and to their neighbors, and is worthy for all its flaws of making such demands. Such an enterprise, we have thought, nourishes our individual spirits and our sociable impulses alike. At the heart of the more than two centuries of American constitutionalism is the conviction that this is an experiment worth continuing.

NOTES

1. 5 U.S. (1 Cranch) 137 (1803). Modern American lawyers often treat *Marbury* as the case that established the power of judicial review, which is historically incorrect but only underlines the symbolic importance of Marshall's opinion. The best recent demolition of the historical legend is William Michael Treanor, Judicial Review Before Marbury, 58 Stan. L. Rev. 455 (2005).

2. 5 U.S. (1 Cranch) at 179–80. The oath of office currently prescribed for federal judges is materially unchanged. See 28 U.S.C. § 453. We can put to one side for present purposes the lively modern debate over just what Marshall thought the power of judicial review encompassed.

3. See, e.g., David A. Strauss, Presidential Interpretation of the Constitution, 15 Cardozo L. Rev. 113, 121 (1993) (describing Marshall's oath argument as "question-begging": "An oath to uphold the Constitution raises—but does not answer—the question: what does the Constitution require?"); Alexander M. Bickel, *The Least Dangerous Branch* 8 (1962) ("Far from supporting Marshall, the oath is perhaps the strongest textual argument against him. For it would seem to obligate each of these officers, in the performance of his own function, to support the Constitution. On one reading, the consequence might be utter chaos—everyone at every juncture interprets and applies the Constitution for himself. Or . . . it may be deduced that everyone is to construe the Constitution with finality insofar as it addresses itself to the performance of his own peculiar function. Surely the language lends itself more readily to this interpretation than to Marshall's apparent conclusion, that everyone's oath to support the Constitution is qualified by the judiciary's oath to do the same, and that every official in government is sworn to support the Constitution as the judges, in pursuance of the same oath, have construed it, rather than as his own conscience may dictate."). This critique is, in fact, an old one. See *Eakin v. Raub*, 12 Serg. & Rawle 330, 352 (Pa. 1825) (Gibson, J., dissenting) ("The oath to support the constitution is not peculiar to the judges, but is taken indiscriminately by every officer of

the government, and is designed rather as a test of the political principles of the man, than to bind the officer in the discharge of his duty").

4. See, e.g., Sanford Levinson, *Constitutional Faith* 75 (1988): "[I]n reading someone, whether friend or foe, one should interpret his or her remarks in a way that maximizes the ability to respect what is being said."

5. 5 U.S. (1 Cranch) at 177.

6. Chief Justice Marshall was not alone in the early Republic in seeing the requirement that state and federal officers take an oath to support the Constitution as creating a moral obligation with respect to the officer's execution of his duties, and not just as a pledge of allegiance to the American political system. One of the most distinguished early commentators on federal constitutional law, William Rawle, held the same view. See Rawle, *A View of the Constitution of the United States of America* 191 (2d ed. 1829) (explaining the constitutionally required oath or affirmation as "a promissory oath [that] greatly increases the moral obligation of the party" with respect to "the duties of the office" and in that respect different from "a general oath of allegiance and fidelity").

7. See H. Jefferson Powell, *A Community Built on Words* 66–73 (2002) (on Marshall and political questions).

8. David P. Bryden, The Lost Union Card, 63 Tul. L. Rev. 1305, 1311 (1989) (summarizing Justice Gibson's argument in *Eakin v. Raub*). Gibson simply disagreed with Marshall and Rawle over the import of the constitutional oath. My suggestion is that we explore the implications of taking the latter seriously.

9. Richard A. Posner, Pragmatism Versus Purposivism in First Amendment Analysis, 54 Stan. L. Rev. 737, 739 (2002).

10. To be fair, Posner has more to say in condemnation of "formalism" than the sentence I have quoted suggests. See, e.g., Richard A. Posner, *Law, Pragmatism, and Democracy* (2003).

11. See, e.g., Henry P. Monaghan, Our Perfect Constitution, 56 N.Y.U. L. Rev. 353, 383–84 (1981): "The authoritative status of the written constitution is a legitimate matter of debate for political theorists interested in the nature of political obligation. That status is, however, an incontestable first principle for theorizing about American constitutional law.... For the purpose of legal reasoning, the binding quality of the constitutional text is itself incapable of and not in need of further demonstration."

12. In a critique of Judge Posner, Jed Rubenfeld remarked that "if any sitting judge other than Richard Posner took th[is] position[] in print, there would be genuine reason to fear for his judicial competence." Rubenfeld, Reply to Posner, 54 Stan. L. Rev. 753, 755 (2002). See also id. at 767 ("I would find it understandable if Congress took the view that a judge

who denies a judicial duty to follow the clear commands of the Constitution or of federal statutes has committed a serious offense.").

13. Posner, *Law, Pragmatism, and Democracy* at 72–73.

14. Rubenfeld, Reply, 54 Stan. L. Rev. at 767.

15. Posner has argued that Marshall was in fact a pragmatist judge . . . rather like Posner. See Posner, *Law, Pragmatism, and Democracy* at 85–93.

16. The Constitution does as well. See U.S. Const. art. I, § 3, cl. 7 ("any Office of honor, Trust, or Profit under the United States"), art. I, § 9, cl. 8 ("any Office of Profit or Trust under [the United States]"), art. II, § 1, cl. 2 ("an Office of Trust or Profit under the United States"), and art. VI, cl. 3("any Office or public Trust under the United States"). The executive branch's application of the passage in Article I, Section 9, which forbids holders of federal "Offices of Profit or Trust" to accept gifts from foreign powers without congressional approval, defines the concept of office of trust in terms of a reciprocal relationship of "trust placed in [the individual]" and a corresponding "undivided loyalty to the United States government." See, e.g., Application of Emoluments Clause to Part-Time Consultant for the Nuclear Regulatory Commission, 10 Op. Off. Legal Counsel 96 (1986).

17. For the founding era, see, e.g., Rawle's discussion in the passage cited above. While my formulation of these presuppositions is exceedingly abstract, I take them, in more concrete versions, to be commonplaces in contemporary American political discourse: seldom discussed because almost always assumed. There are big philosophical and theological issues lurking just barely under the surface here. I think we can leave them to one side because of the existence of a meaningful social consensus about the surface (superficial?) propositions.

18. See generally Stuart Hampshire, *Justice Is Conflict* 6–48 (2000). The quotations are from pages 28 and 26.

19. In all likelihood this way of putting it is actually backward: Hampshire, an Englishman who spent a great deal of time in the United States, almost certainly had the American system partly in mind in devising his general theory.

20. "X is (un)constitutional because that is God's will" and "X is (un)constitutional because a majority in my party prefer that conclusion" are not wrong forms of constitutional reasoning so much as they are simply not constitutional reasoning at all. No one wishing to be taken seriously on a constitutional matter would offer them as arguments, however relevant or controlling either may be for some people in other settings.

21. Judge Posner himself represents a rather pure and unsparing example of this perspective, which others often entertain in softer forms. See, e.g.,

Richard A. Posner, *The Problematics of Moral and Legal Theory* (1999), esp. at 258 (courts properly "treat the Constitution and the common law ... as a kind of putty that can be used to fill embarrassing holes in the legal and political framework of society"). The locus classicus for the claim that moral language is misleading in legal analysis is the famous article by Justice Oliver Wendell Holmes, Jr., The Path of the Law, 10 Harv. L. Rev. 167 (1897). Holmes, however, had a strong sense of the obligations attendant on judicial decision and an equally strong objection to any assumption on a court's part that it was authorized to invoke the Constitution as a justification for addressing what the justices thought wrong (or even embarrassing) in law or society. Holmes, in other words, was an anti-instrumentalist in constitutional law. See, e.g., *Lochner v. New York*, 198 U.S. 45, 75 (1905) (Holmes, J. dissenting) ("[T]he accident of our finding certain opinions [embodied in law] natural and familiar, or novel, and even shocking, ought not to conclude our judgment upon the question whether statutes embodying them conflict with the Constitution of the United States").

22. The position I am criticizing should not be confused with the "moral reading" of the Constitution proposed by the distinguished philosopher of law Ronald Dworkin. See Dworkin, *Freedom's Law: The Moral Reading of the American Constitution* (1996). Dworkin himself does not hold the essentially emotivist understanding of moral discourse to which I am referring. The position I lay out in this book, in fact, overlaps in part with his concept of law as integrity, see Dworkin, *Law's Empire* (1986), although Dworkin develops his concept into a substantive theory about what decision makers should do, while my concern is primarily with how to understand the moral situation in which they decide. On emotivism (the assumption that conflicting moral positions are expressions of nonrational preferences that cannot be argued, but only asserted), see Alasdair MacIntyre, *After Virtue* 6-35 (2d ed. 1984).

23. I mean to allude to Sanford Levinson's seminal book *Constitutional Faith* (1988), which remains crucial to any attempt to understand the relationship between moral commitment and American constitutionalism. Levinson also discussed the oath passage in *Marbury*, in id. at 92-93 and 122-23.

24. In the early twenty-first century the Court has by a very large margin the loudest institutional voice in constitutional debate. Whether that is as it should be is another question, but being a fact it justifies an investigation that mostly ignores lower-court and state-court judges (among whose moral circumstances is their position in the judicial hierarchy) and gives only glancing attention to the position of nonjudicial officials (whose express immersion in partisan politics creates a sharp contrast with the

official role of judges), despite the enormously important role all of these play in the American constitutional order.

CHAPTER ONE

1. Mark Tushnet, Themes in Warren Court Biographies, 70 N.Y.U. L. Rev. 748, 763 (1995).

2. James F. Simon, *The Center Holds: The Power Struggle Inside the Rehnquist Court* 54 (1995).

3. R. Ted Cruz, In Memoriam: William H. Rehnquist, 119 Harv. L. Rev. 10, 15 (2005).

4. My qualification is meant to acknowledge that the late Chief Justice William H. Rehnquist's opinions on abortion regulation, from his dissent in *Roe* on, called for the Court to review such regulations for their rationality and thus acknowledged (explicitly in *Roe*) that there could be abortion laws that the Court should strike down. See *Roe v. Wade*, 410 U.S. 113, 173 (1973) (Rehnquist, J., dissenting) (suggesting that a prohibitory statute with no exception for situations involving risk to the mother's life would be irrational).

5. Finley Peter Dunne, *Mr. Dooley's Opinions* 26 (1900).

6. There are many accounts. See, e.g., Lucas A. Powe, Jr., *The Warren Court and American Politics* 21–74 (2000).

7. See, e.g., Gregory A. Caldeira & James L. Gibson, The Etiology of Public Support for the Supreme Court, 36 Am. J. Pol. Sci. 635 (1992).

8. It may seem coy to ignore *Bush v. Gore* at this point, but I do not want to get sidetracked on that interesting but distractingly hot-button example. Suffice it to say that the justices' unanimous willingness to involve themselves in a case as (apparently) tailor made to bring the Court into disrepute with half the country and the fact that their decision had no lasting effect on public opinion support the position I take in the text. See, e.g., L. Michael Seidman, What's So Bad About *Bush v. Gore*? An Essay on Our Unsettled Election, 47 Wayne L. Rev. 953, 960 (2001) ("Public opinion polls suggested that, even though many people (correctly) understood that Bush v. Gore was political, the Court paid no price for the decision and may have even benefited from it.") (citation omitted); id. at 960 n. 16 ("A variety of polls found that the Court's standing with the American public changed little after its decision.").

9. Some readers may feel that our fictional justices are modeled on actual constitutionalists. While that is not in fact my intention, there are certain broad resemblances. Justice John has no parallel even remotely similar. When critics of the Court attack individual justices, what they describe is roughly what Justice Johanna privately understands herself to

hold: she corresponds to polemics, not to the actual views of any justice except, perhaps Abe Fortas. See n. 11 below. Some readers may see Justices Black and Scalia in our Justice Oliver, and if they do, they may also find Justice Marsha to resemble Justice Brennan. I think any similarities are, at most, however, caricatures.

10. Indeed, such practical considerations conceivably might bring Justice John a reputation for intellectual distinction on the Court. See David Daube's classic article, A Corrupt Judge Sets the Pace (1984), reprinted in Daube, *Collected Studies in Roman Law* 1379–94 (David Cohen & Dieter Simon ed., 1991).

11. It has been suggested that Justice Brennan's colleague Abe Fortas viewed his role in this manner. See Tushnet, Themes, 70 N.Y.U. L. Rev. at 754–58, discussing Laura Kalman, *Abe Fortas: A Biography* (1990). Fortas himself came to judicial shipwreck because of conduct somewhat akin to that of Justice John.

12. Compare Richard A. Posner, *Breaking the Deadlock* 128 (2001) (the equal-protection rationale on the basis of which the Court stated that it was deciding *Bush v. Gore* "is not a persuasive ground" for the decision), with id. at 168 (the justices who joined in Chief Justice Rehnquist's concurrence were right to join in the equal-protection-based opinion of the Court even if they did not find it plausible). See also id. at 166–67 (Justice Scalia was "ill advised to go public" with his actual views on the case).

13. He need not subscribe to arguments that there is a single right answer in such cases as opposed to an answer that, considering all the relevant and legitimate legal arguments, appears to be the best.

14. 3 U.S. (3 Dall.) 386, 397 (1798) (seriatim opinion of Paterson, J.).

15. *Roper v. Simmons*, 543 U.S. 551, 607–08 (2005) (dissenting opinion joined by three justices) (citations omitted). Lest the reader fear that this sort of language is used only on one side of the Court's divisions, read the following, from a different perspective:

> The document that the plurality construes today is unfamiliar to me. It is not the living charter that I have taken to be our Constitution; it is instead a stagnant, archaic, hidebound document steeped in the prejudices and superstitions of a time long past. This Constitution does not recognize that times change, does not see that sometimes a practice or rule outlives its foundations. I cannot accept an interpretive method that does such violence to the charter that I am bound by oath to uphold.

Michael H. v. Gerald D., 491 U.S. 110, 141 (1989) (dissenting opinion joined by three justices).

16. Justice Brennan was perhaps of this view. Brennan "was once asked what he did when the law seemed to suggest one answer and justice another. Thinking for a moment, he responded, 'I don't recall ever having such a case.'" Shirley S. Abrahamson, Susan Craighead & Daniel N. Abrahamson, Words and Sentences: Penalty Enhancement for Hate Crimes, 16 U. Ark. Little Rock L. J. 515, 532 n. 51 (1994), quoting discussion in Seminar, Georgetown University Law Center (Fall 1993).

17. I discuss this nonjudicial case at greater length in H. Jefferson Powell, *A Community Built on Words* 11–21 (2002). To anticipate a question the next sentence in the text may raise, there was no discernible original intent or meaning about the question other than what could be inferred from the text of the appointments clause (which was effectively zero). Jefferson himself implied that the legal concept of separation of powers supported his conclusion, but given the discrepancy between his account of the concept (exceptions to a rigid separation are to be narrowly construed) and that of other founders such as Madison (who defined the appropriate separation as existing as long as the entire function of one branch of government is not usurped by another), this was hardly a conclusive argument. On Madison's view, see *The Federalist* No. 47, at 325–26 (Jacob E. Cooke ed., 1961).

18. See generally Barry Friedman, The Politics of Judicial Review, 84 Tex. L. Rev. 257 (2005), and the studies Friedman cites.

19. See Philip Bobbitt, *Constitutional Interpretation* 86–108 (1991).

20. See James Madison, Letter to Charles Jared Ingersoll (June 25, 1831), in *The Mind of the Founder* 390–93 (Marvin Meyers rev. ed., 1981). Madison explained that his decision in 1816 to sign into law the bill creating the second national bank did not indicate a change in his "solitary opinions" on the best reading of Article I, but stemmed from his conviction that the repeated endorsement of the constitutionality of the first national bank by Congress, the executive, and the courts "amount[ed] to the requisite evidence of the national judgment and intention" about the Constitution's public meaning.

21. See Friedman, Politics of Judicial Review, 84 Tex. L. Rev. at 257.

22. See Henry P. Monaghan, Our Perfect Constitution, 56 N.Y.U.L. Rev. 353 (1981).

23. She explains her respect for stare decisis along similar lines, but we need not explore the details, except to note that in light of the importance of the Rule of Five power to the execution of the Constitution as she understands it, some degree of respect for precedent plays a part in her consideration of the humanly best outcome in many cases: a general abandonment of the Court's modest willingness to adhere to precedent would have very substantial adverse effects on its ability to play its role.

24. The fact that equal protection is not an express textual guarantee against the federal government might be thought to render the equal-protection argument even more farcical: an attempt to override clear constitutional text by a nontextual principle. See *Seminole Tribe of Florida v. Florida*, 517 U.S. 44, 116 (1996) (Souter, J., dissenting): the "plain text is the Man of Steel in a confrontation with 'background principle[s]' and 'postulates which limit and control.'"

25. Justice Marsha is inclined to put this last point as given in the text but thinks it equally sensible to treat the issue as nuancing the Constitution's mandate to reach the best outcome as actually being to "reach the best outcome except where no sensible person would think the text of the relevant provision amenable to that outcome."

26. I have in mind provisions such as the ex post facto clauses of Article I, Sections 9 and 10. The language of the clauses looks rather specific but in fact has a latent ambiguity—do the clauses apply to civil laws with retrospective effect as well as to retrospective changes in criminal law? The Court's answer, since its very early decision in *Calder v. Bull*, 3 U.S. (3 Dall.) 386 (1798), has been to resolve the ambiguity against applying the clauses to civil legislation. But see *E. Enterprises v. Apfel*, 524 U.S. 498, 539 (1998) (Thomas, J., concurring) ("In an appropriate case . . . I would be willing to reconsider Calder and its progeny to determine whether a retroactive civil law . . . is . . . unconstitutional under the Ex Post Facto Clause"). I discuss *Calder* in Powell, *A Community Built on Words* at 43–52.

27. The quotation is from Charles Evans Hughes, *Addresses of Charles Evans Hughes* 185 (1916). Chief Justice Hughes came to regret his comment. See Hughes, *The Autobiographical Notes of Charles Evans Hughes* 143–44 (1973).

28. Patrick McK. Brennan, Locating Authority in Law, in *Civilizing Authority* 169 (Patrick McK. Brennan ed., 2007).

29. See, e.g., Stuart Hampshire, *Justice Is Conflict* 31 (2000): "All modern societies are, to a greater or lesser degree, morally mixed, with rival conceptions of justice, conservative and radical, flaring into open conflict and needing arbitration." John Rawls, *Justice as Fairness: A Restatement* 33 (2001): "[W]e assume the fact of reasonable pluralism to be a permanent condition of a democratic society."

30. Another big issue in the philosophy of ethics lurks here, though I do not need to take a position on it: Is deep ethical conflict essentially and incorrigibly universal in our society, or is it possible through some sort of overlapping consensus or moral bricolage to establish areas of agreement on particular but broad areas of moral concern? See, e.g., Rawls, *Justice* at 32–33 (a reasonable overlapping consensus is the best "basis of political

and social unity" in a liberal democracy); Jeffrey Stout, *Ethics After Babel* 240–42 (2d ed. 2001) (moral bricolage permits a morally pluralistic society to draw ethical lines "here or there in countless particular cases"). In any event, it is undeniable that our society has broad areas of profound moral disagreement that bear on constitutional law.

CHAPTER TWO

1. Learned Hand, *The Spirit of Liberty* 306–07 (Irving Dilliard ed., 3d ed. 1960).

2. See Oliver Wendell Holmes, Jr., The Path of the Law, 10 Harv. L. Rev. 167 (1897).

3. Just to be clear, in this book I use the term "ethical" in the ordinary English sense, not as Philip Bobbitt does, to refer to constitutional arguments based on the American ethos of limited government.

4. Grant Gilmore, *The Ages of American Law* 49 (1977).

5. See Michael Herz, "Do Justice!": Variations of a Thrice-Told Tale, 82 Va. L. Rev. 111, 111, 146 (1996). Professor Herz's article is an outstanding piece of academic detective work.

6. See Mark Tushnet, *Red, White, and Blue* 108 (1988). Professor Herz found several other versions that recount Holmes's statement along substantially the same lines.

7. Herz agrees with Philip Bobbitt that "'[t]here is a world of difference between, on the one hand, trying conscientiously to play by the rules and, on the other hand, seeing your task as making others do so.' The latter implies an unempathetic haughtiness and a freedom from the rules for oneself. At best, this is the petty bureaucrat's unthinking rule fetishism; at worst it is a cynical and dictatorial abuse of authority." Herz, "Do Justice!", 82 Va. L. Rev. at 135, quoting Philip Bobbitt, Is Law Politics?, 41 Stan. L. Rev. 1233, 1301 (1989).

8. Herz, "Do Justice!", 82 Va. L. Rev. at 130. The altruism phrase is from Oliver Wendell Holmes, Jr., Letter to Lewis Einstein (July 17, 1909), in *The Holmes-Einstein Letters* 48 (James B. Peabody ed., 1964). Holmes used the metaphor or paired metaphors of "the game" and "playing by the rules" elsewhere as well. See, e.g., Holmes, Letter to Einstein at 45 (playing "the game"); Holmes, Law and the Court (1913), in *The Essential Holmes* 145 (Richard A. Posner ed., 1992) ("solving a problem according to the rules").

9. If I am right to read Holmes in this manner, what Hand meant in using the do-justice anecdote as a gloss on Holmes's harsh "I hate justice" becomes clear. The latter was simply Holmes's severe and typically provocative way of putting, in aphoristic form, the view I ascribe to him.

10. Alan Watson, *Authority of Law, and Law* 143 (2003).

11. Charles Evans Hughes, *Addresses of Charles Evans Hughes* 185 (1916).

12. Charles Evans Hughes, *The Autobiographical Notes of Charles Evans Hughes* 143–44 (1973).

13. John Hart Ely, *Democracy and Distrust* 221 n. 4 (1980). Ely might have seen some of the examples Justice Marsha has in mind as cases of textual ambiguity, Secretary Jefferson's issue (for example) being one of how to interpret the appointments clause of Article II. That seems to me a less helpful way of thinking about Jefferson's question, which concerned not what to make of the words of the clause but what to do about an issue that the words did not in themselves address in any linguistic fashion. But this is probably quibbling over how to characterize a fact about the Constitution on which Ely, Marsha, and I agree: there are many important questions in constitutional law that "surely require[] the injection of content not found in the document." Id. at 41 n. *.

14. As my quotation is meant to remind us, Professor Ely cheerfully admitted that *Democracy and Distrust* was broadly speaking an explication of Justice Harlan Fiske Stone's famous footnote 4 in *United States v. Carolene Products Co.*, as well as an apologia for the work of the Supreme Court under Chief Justice Earl Warren, to whom Ely dedicated his book.

15. Ely, *Democracy and Distrust* at 221 n. 4. Ely labeled such provisions "the Constitution's more directive provisions."

16. There is a substantial argument that it was Alexander M. Bickel, in his 1962 book *The Least Dangerous Branch*, who really ought to be given the credit here. In light of the fact that Bickel later came to doubt much of his own argument, he might well prefer that we saddle Ely with the responsibility.

17. See, e.g., Melvyn R. Durchslag, The Supreme Court and the Federalist Papers: Is There Less Here Than Meets the Eye?, 14 Wm. & Mary Bill Rts. J. 243 (2005); Ira C. Lupu, Time, the Supreme Court, and The Federalist, 66 Geo. Wash. L. Rev. 1324 (1998).

18. 1 Joseph Story, *Commentaries on the Constitution of the United States* 389 (1833).

19. I should note the logical possibility that some theory will someday come down the pike that is so persuasive that it garners lasting support from the Court, the profession, and the public. If that were to happen, we might conclude that "the people" had adopted it, informally, as the right theory of judicial review. We can worry about whether to think so when it happens.

20. Robert H. Jackson, *The Supreme Court in the American System of Government* 55–56 (1955).

21. *Kamper v. Hawkins*, 3 Va. (1 Va. Cas.) 20, 39 (Va. Gen. Ct. 1793) (seriatim opinion).

22. *League of United Latin Am. Citizens v. Clements*, 914 F.2d 620, 628 (5th Cir. 1990) (en banc), rev'd, 501 U.S. 419 (1991). The Supreme Court's decision reversing the appeals court did not reject or indeed discuss the lower court's description of the role of the judge.

23. 408 U.S. 238, 410–11 (1972) (Blackmun, J., dissenting). Blackmun later changed his mind about the death penalty. See *Callins v. Collins,* 510 U.S. 1141, 1145–46 (1994) (Blackmun, J., dissenting).

24. See Mark B. Rotenburg, Politics, Personality and Judging: The Lessons of Brandeis and Frankfurter on Judicial Review, 83 Colum. L. Rev. 1863, 1863 n.1 (1983).

25. *The Federalist* No. 51, at 349 (Jacob E. Cooke ed., 1961).

26. Bobbitt's first iteration of the argument came out at almost exactly the same time as Ely's *Democracy and Distrust*. See Philip Bobbitt, *Constitutional Fate: Theory of the Constitution*, which appeared in book form in 1982, two years after *Democracy and Distrust*, although the public lectures on which Bobbitt drew were given in 1979. See the law review presentation of Bobbitt's lectures at 58 Tex. L. Rev. 695 (1980). Bobbitt further developed his approach in his *Constitutional Interpretation* (1991). Although Bobbitt's analysis of the forms of constitutional argument has been widely influential, it has been Ely's form of constitutional theory that has dominated the academic discussion.

27. Bobbitt, *Constitutional Interpretation* at 186.

28. Id. at 24.

29. Id. at 5.

30. Id. at 4–5, 121.

31. Professor Bobbitt's typology of the archetypal modalities of common-law argument—historical, textual, doctrinal, prudential, structural, and ethical (as in "ethos," not morality per se)—has often been discussed, and I will not repeat those analyses here. There is, to be sure, nothing sacred or philosophically fundamental about these forms of argument, and over time they may (and occasionally do) change. As a general matter, however, the overall set of recognized forms of argument has remained remarkably stable since the founding era.

32. Id. at 24.

33. Id. at 22.

34. Bobbitt's invocation of conscience in the resolution of constitutional questions where arguments based on different modalities clash has been criticized on basically these lines. See Gene R. Nichol, Constitutional Judgment, 91 Mich. L. Rev. 1107, 1115-16 (1993). I attempted to show why

this criticism misunderstands Bobbitt's position in H. Jefferson Powell, Constitutional Investigations, 72 Tex. L. Rev. 1731 (1994).

CHAPTER THREE

1. It was not even clear at first that the attorney general ought to be considered a member of the president's inner council, although within a few years the first attorney general, Edmund Randolph, was regularly attending cabinet meetings at President Washington's request. Attorney General Caleb Cushing ended the tradition of maintaining a private practice in 1854 after Congress raised the office's compensation to match that of the executive department heads. See Office and Duties of Attorney General, 6 Op. Att'y Gen. 326, 354 (1854).

2. Though these tasks remain vested as a formal matter in the attorney general, they are now performed in practice almost exclusively by subordinate officials within the Justice Department, in particular by the assistant attorney general who heads the Office of Legal Counsel. I should note that I served in that office in various capacities during the 1990s and that my perspective on executive-branch lawyering is shaped by that experience.

3. I have relied for these details primarily on the classic book by Attorney General Homer Cummings and Carl McFarland, *Federal Justice: Chapters in the History of Justice and the Federal Executive* (1937). In creating the Department of Justice, the act of 1870 made the attorney general's advisory role a constitutional one: Article II, Section 2, of the Constitution provides that the president "may require the Opinion, in writing, of the principal Officer in each of the executive Departments, upon any Subject relating to the Duties of their respective Offices."

4. Akerman was a remarkable person, and a man of great moral courage as well as a skilled lawyer. President Grant's biographer, William S. McFeely, has noted that "[t]here is astonishingly little biographical information on Akerman," and his own writings are the main exception to this "conspiracy of historical silence." McFeely, *Grant: A Biography* 367 (1981). See id. at 366–74; McFeely, "Amos T. Akerman: The Lawyer and Racial Justice," in *Region, Race, and Reconstruction* 395–415 (J. Morgan Kousser & James M. McPherson eds., 1982). Akerman was a New Hampshire native, but he moved to Georgia after college, and when the Civil War came, he fought on the side of the Confederacy. After the war, Akerman played an active part in trying to build up a regional Republican party in the South and was appointed U.S. attorney for Georgia in 1869; a year later, President Grant made Akerman the first Southerner to serve in Grant's cabinet,

from his appointment in June 1870 until his resignation at Grant's request in January 1872. Akerman was a vigorous and effective administrator who took with utter seriousness his, and the federal government's, obligation to enforce the Civil War amendments and the civil rights legislation which Congress had enacted to implement those amendments. As he explained to a friend while in office, Akerman believed the South's "surrender in good faith really" ought to involve "a surrender of the substance as well as of the forms of the Confederate cause," and Akerman's zeal in enforcing the constitutional and statutory provisions protecting African Americans suggests that he was sincere in doing so. Some modern scholars think, indeed, that Akerman came to be seen as too dedicated to racial equality and that this may have played a role in Grant's decision to seek his resignation, although it is also likely that Akerman's active investigation of corruption in the railroad industry led to pressure on Grant for his removal. See Amos T. Akerman, Letter to James Jackson (Nov. 20, 1871), quoted in Lou Falkner Williams, *The Great South Carolina Ku Klux Klan Trials, 1871–1872* 44 (1996). Williams's superb book is a careful study of the effort by the Justice Department and local federal officials in South Carolina to suppress the KKK, an effort which Akerman played a major role in instigating and, up to his resignation, in supervising. Id. at 61.

5. Civil-Service Commission, 13 Op. Att'y Gen. 516 (1871). Akerman described the relevant statute in the second paragraph of his opinion:

> That commission has been appointed under the 9th section of the act of March 3, 1871, making appropriations for sundry civil expenses of the Government for the year ending June 30, 1872, and for other purposes, which is as follows: "That the President of the United States be, and he is hereby, authorized to prescribe such rules and regulations for the admission of persons into the civil service of the United States as will best promote the efficiency thereof, and ascertain the fitness of each candidate in respect to age, health, character, knowledge, and ability for the branch of service into which he seeks to enter; and for this purpose the President is authorized to employ suitable persons to conduct said inquiries, to prescribe their duties, and to establish regulations for the conduct of persons who may receive appointments in the civil service" (16 Stat., 514.)

6. In Akerman's words,

> if the President, authorized by an act of Congress, should prescribe that the courts and heads of Departments should always appoint the persons named by a civil-service board, that board would virtually be the appointing power, and that act of Congress would be the foundation of its authority.

7. See Promotion of Marine Officer, 68 Op. Att'y Gen. 291, 292–93 (1956).

8. *Morrison v. Olson*, 487 U.S. 654, 703 (1988) (Scalia, J., dissenting).

9. The distinction between "officers" and "employees" was already an old and settled one, the seminal judicial precedent being a decision by Chief Justice Marshall which Akerman cited early in his opinion. See *United States v. Maurice*, 26 F. Cas. 1211 (C.C.D.Va. 1823).

10. "And these provisions must be construed as excluding all other modes of appointment." Why was Akerman so peremptory? Since he does not explain, we can only speculate, but there are a couple of obvious and mutually supporting possibilities. It is an old principle of interpretation in common law courts that *expressio unius exclusio alterius*—if a document says A, B, and C, it should ordinarily be interpreted not to mean D as well. In the early Republic, this interpretive rule of thumb became linked in constitutional law with the proposition that the Constitution is supreme law, a set of mandates binding on all three branches of the federal government rather a collection of default rules subject to variance at Congress's, or anyone else's, choice. The very language of the appointments clause itself, against this background, might have suggested to Akerman that its list of the possible "repositaries" of the power to appoint must be exclusive, since the clause expressly provides Congress with discretion ("as they think proper") on the separate question of when to vest the appointment of inferior officers other than in the president-with-Senate-approval.

11. I have not found any opinion in which Akerman cited Story, but it is very difficult to believe that he was not familiar with the treatise; in any event, Akerman's discussion echoes Story's much longer treatment of the subject. See 3 Joseph Story, *Commentaries on the Constitution of the United States* 372–412 (1833). William Rawle's treatise, also widely used in the first part of the nineteenth century, took a similar view of the purpose of the Constitution's arrangements. See Rawle, *A View of the Constitution of the United States of America* 150–53 (1825).

12. At this point, Akerman seems to suggest that working backward from the clear linguistic significance of "Advice and Consent," we can conclude that "nominate" and "appoint" cannot be "merely nominal either," but he makes nothing more of this.

13. See *Veazie Bank v. Fenno*, 75 U.S. 533 (8 Wall.) 533, 544 (1869).

14. Akerman cited *United States v. Hartwell*, 73 U.S. (6 Wall.) 385, 393–94 (1868).

15. Few sophisticated lawyers would agree with a bald statement that the justices of the Supreme Court, for example, are dispassionate and neu-

tral, but it is remarkable that the same lawyers who would sagely agree about the justices' political orientations can then turn around and make assumptions about issues such as the proper relationship between the courts and the political branches which seem to rest on the dispassionate-and-neutral paradigm.

16. 4 John Marshall, *Life of George Washington* 243 (reprint 1983) (1805).

17. See generally James Boyd White, *Living Speech: Resisting the Empire of Force* (2006).

18. For anyone curious about the upshot of Akerman's advice, the rules which the commission finally submitted to the president took some account of his constitutional concern: appointments not exempt from the rules were to be filled by the appointing authority choosing from among the three candidates who scored highest on the competitive examination. President Grant submitted the rules to Congress with a promise to implement them on his own and a request that Congress enact legislation to make the reforms permanent. Ulysses S. Grant, Message to the Senate and House of Representatives (Dec. 19, 1871), in 6 *Messages and Papers of the Presidents* 4110–13 (James D. Richardson ed., 1897) (including the "Rules for the Civil Service" as an appendix). Congress failed to do so, and at the end of 1874 Grant informed Congress that he would abandon the rules without affirmative legislation. Similar reforms became the law in 1883. See Ulysses S. Grant III, *Ulysses S. Grant: Warrior and Statesman* 312–13 (1969).

19. See Henry P. Monaghan, Our Perfect Constitution, 56 N.Y.U. L. Rev. 353 (1981).

20. Though perhaps not quite impossible. The great antislavery constitutionalist Frederick Douglass made the attempt on the eve of the Civil War. See Douglass, The Constitution of the United States: Is It Pro-Slavery or Anti-Slavery? (May 26,1860), in 2 *Life and Writings of Frederick Douglass* 467–80 (Philip S. Foner ed., 1975).

21. There is, I should note, another problem quite the opposite of that posed by the perfect-Constitution thesis: the risk that lawyers will treat the Constitution as their exclusive preserve, and constitutional law as so technical a discipline that the unwashed laity cannot be thought to understand it. The worry that this can happen and the perception (with which I completely agree) that it is a threat to our system are old. One of Akerman's most distinguished predecessors, Hugh Swinton Legaré, charged the Marshall Court with this error in the 1820s. See Legaré, Book Review, in 2 *Writings of Hugh Swinton Legaré* 102 (M. Legare ed., 1845), originally published in 2 S. Rev. (Aug. 1828), at 72. We live in an era not especially prone to this

sort of mistake, I think, and I believe that the best technical constitutional lawyers have always striven to make their arguments open to any intelligent reader. The proper role of technical argument in constitutional law is not to create obscurity.

22. See Lincoln Caplan, *The Tenth Justice: The Solicitor General and the Rule of Law* (1987).

23. See Nancy V. Baker, *Conflicting Loyalties* 143, 150, 145 (1992).

24. Justice Hugo Black made a similar point in his opinion for the Supreme Court in *United States v. South-Eastern Underwriters Ass'n*, 322 U.S. 533, 549 n. 31 (1944):

> That different members of the Court applying th[e relevant doctrinal] test to a particular state statute may reach opposite conclusions as to its validity does not argue against the correctness of the test itself. Such differences in judgment are inevitable where solution of a Constitutional problem must depend upon considered evaluation of competing Constitutional objectives.

CHAPTER FOUR

1. Alasdair MacIntyre, *After Virtue* 263 (2d ed. 1984). To be precise, the passage occurs on the last page of the first edition.

2. Id. at 253.

3. To be fair, MacIntyre does remark that the Court can "display[] a fairness which consists in even-handedness in its adjudications," which appears to concede some minimal moral content to its truce-keeping function. I am inclined to think that he meant nothing more than that the Court cannot appear to favor one side in a social conflict so strongly that the other has nothing to gain from accepting the truce the justices negotiate, but the discussion is very brief and somewhat cryptic.

4. As the reader already knows, I believe that the argument I am presenting applies to political-branch lawyers, mutatis mutandis, as much as to those public servants who are lawyers with black robes. The reservation expressed by the Latin tag is not trivial—see chapter 3—but the general point is as stated in English. I shall not clutter the text with reminders that it is not only the justices whose decisions bear moral weight in constitutional matters, or that the exact manner in which the moral considerations play depends on within which branch of government the lawyer serves.

5. MacIntyre's *After Virtue* is a seminal and central work in the rediscovery of a virtue-based approach to ethics, and I do not wish my disagreements with him to obscure the great debt I owe to his writings.

6. I am profoundly indebted to Joseph Vining for showing me how legal argument necessarily rests on moral presuppositions. See, e.g., Vining, *From Newton's Sleep* (1995).

7. 252 U.S. 416, 433–34 (1920): "[W]hen we are dealing with words that also are a constituent act, like the Constitution of the United States, we must realize that they have called into life a being the development of which could not have been foreseen completely by the most gifted of its begetters. It was enough for them to realize or to hope that they had created an organism; it has taken a century and has cost their successors much sweat and blood to prove that they created a nation. The case before us must be considered in the light of our whole experience and not merely in that of what was said a hundred years ago. . . . We must consider what this country has become in deciding" the operative meaning of constitutional language.

8. In this context, it is ironic that MacIntyre is a leading proponent in recent moral philosophy of the proposition that meaningful, rational conversation can be carried on under conditions of serious disagreement about moral and political issues. MacIntyre has strongly defended the concept of a moral tradition central to his thinking against the charge that it amounts to rule by lifeless or unchanging taboos: a living moral tradition is characterized by ongoing disagreement over what should be said about the goals and practices of the tradition. See *After Virtue* at 163–64, 221–22. See also his discussion of "the necessary place of conflict within traditions" in Alasdair MacIntyre, *Whose Justice? Which Rationality?* 11 and passim (1988).

9. See generally Vining, *From Newton's Sleep*, and especially pages 145–47.

10. On Justice Black's understanding of constitutional interpretation, see David Lange & H. Jefferson Powell, *No Law: Intellectual Property in the Image of an Absolute First Amendment* (forthcoming 2008), especially part 3, chapter 4.

11. Writing specifically about the meaning of the Fourteenth Amendment, Justice Harlan claimed that "[d]ue process has not been reduced to any formula; its content cannot be determined by reference to any code. The best that can be said is that through the course of this Court's decisions it has represented the balance which our Nation, built upon postulates of respect for the liberty of the individual, has struck between that liberty and the demands of organized society. . . . The balance of which I speak is the balance struck by this country, having regard to what history teaches are the traditions from which it developed as well as the traditions from which it broke. That tradition is a living thing." *Poe v. Ullman*, 367 U.S. 497, 542 (1961) (Harlan, J., dissenting). The subsequent quotations in the text are from the same dissent, id. at 543 and 544, respectively.

12. *Adamson v. People of State of California*, 332 U.S. 46, 90, 92 (1947) (Black, J. dissenting). See as well Black's opinion for the Court in *United States v. South-Eastern Underwriters Ass'n*, where he noted that "differences in judgment are inevitable where solution of a Constitutional problem must depend upon considered evaluation of competing Constitutional objectives." 322 U.S. 533, 549 n. 31 (1944).

13. Roger K. Newman, The Warren Court and American Politics: An Impressionistic Appreciation, 18 Const. Comment. 661, 667 n. 29 (2002), quoting an interview with Joseph Price.

14. *The Federalist* No. 37, at 236 (Jacob E. Cooke ed., 1961).

15. *United States v. Kahriger*, 345 U.S. 22, 34 (1953) (Jackson, J., concurring); *Edwards v. California*, 314 U.S. 160, 183 (1941) (Jackson, J., concurring). The quotations in the following paragraph are from *Youngstown Sheet & Tube Co. v. Sawyer*, 343 U.S. 579, 634–35 (1952) (Jackson, J., concurring).

16. See generally James Boyd White, *Living Speech: Resisting the Empire of Force* (2006).

17. It is important to acknowledge once again Ronald Dworkin's use of a concept of integrity in a sense that overlaps somewhat with my own. Compare the current discussion with Dworkin's in his important book *Law's Empire* (1986), esp. at 176–90. The constitutional virtue of integrity that I am describing is perhaps closer to what Dworkin terms "the interpretive attitude." Id. at 46–49.

18. See *Helvering v. Gregory*, 69 F.2d 809, 810 (2d Cir. 1934) (L. Hart, Cir. J.) ("Anyone may so arrange his affairs so that his taxes shall be as low as possible; he is not bound to chose that pattern which will best pay the Treasury; there is not even a patriotic duty to increase one's taxes."), aff'd, 293 U.S. 465 (1935). Despite Judge Hand's vigorous defense of tax avoidance, he concluded in *Gregory* that the taxpayer had failed to pay "her just taxes." 69 F.2d at 811. I am grateful to Professor Richard Schmalbeck for guiding me to this famous opinion.

19. In this regard, Judge Posner's view of the role of constitutional law is instructive: the courts should "treat the Constitution and the common law . . . as a kind of putty that can be used to fill embarrassing holes in the legal and political framework of society." Richard A. Posner, *The Problematics of Moral and Legal Theory* 258 (1999). See also Posner, *Law, Pragmatism, and Democracy* 48–49 (2003), where he discusses the choice of formalist or nonformalist rhetoric in the presentation of a constitutional decision as a question of which is more effective. The choice, it seems, has nothing to do with the actual grounds of decision.

It should be clear that in denying the coherence within an instrumentalist perspective of the constitutional virtue of integrity I am saying nothing derogatory about the personal integrity of Posner or any other instrumentalist. Justice Johanna, the reader will recall, is personally incorruptible and sincerely believes that she makes the best decisions for society. The constitutional virtues are habits or dispositions with respect to playing the constitutional game. That said, I suggest below that the cultivation of the constitutional virtues is conducive to broader, more humane patterns of public conduct generally.

20. *The Federalist* No. 10, at 57–58.

21. The Constitution's dictates with respect to religion are especially complex. On the one hand, it is clear that all citizens are entitled to participate fully in public life without regard to their religious beliefs. On the other, the First Amendment expressly forbids at least some ways of interjecting religion into public life and the law (government "shall make no law respecting an establishment of religion"). The Constitution thus demands that public actors avoid using government as a tool of religious faith while guaranteeing their right to serve in the public sphere without (as it were) leaving their faith at the door. There is no abstract solution to the reconciliation of these demands, but the constitutional virtue of integrity makes it possible to live them out in practice.

22. What I am calling the constitutional virtue of humility is very close to what Judge Learned Hand termed "the spirit of liberty," "the spirit which is not too sure that it is right." Hand, *The Spirit of Liberty* 190 (Irving Dilliard ed., 3d ed. 1960).

23. 187 U.S. 606, 608–09 (1903).

24. 198 U.S. 45, 76 (1905) (Holmes, J., dissenting).

25. 319 U.S. 624, 642 (1943).

26. James Madison, Letter to Charles Jared Ingersoll (June 25, 1831), in *The Mind of the Founder* (Marvin Meyers rev. ed., 1981), at 392.

27. Id.

28. Oliver Wendell Holmes, Jr., Letter to Alice Stopford Green (August 20, 1909), in *The Essential Holmes* 116 (Richard A. Posner ed., 1992).

CHAPTER FIVE

1. 501 U.S. 529 (1991). There was no opinion of the Court, the six justices who concurred in the judgment producing a total of four opinions and at least three rationales. The new rule of law in question in *Beam* was a constitutional one, announced by the Supreme Court in *Bacchus Imports, Ltd. v. Dias*, 468

U.S. 263 (1984) (holding that a state tax on liquor sales that discriminates in favor of locally produced beverages violates the commerce clause).

2. 501 U.S. at 549 (Scalia, J., concurring in the judgment) (citation omitted), quoting *Marbury v. Madison*, 5 U.S. (1 Cranch) 137, 177 (1803). The emphases are Justice Scalia's.

3. 501 U.S. at 546-47 (White, J., concurring in the judgment); Jeffrey Toobin, *The Nine* 97 (2007) (quoting O'Connor).

4. *Ollman v. Evans*, 750 F.2d 970, 994 (D.C. Cir. 1984) (Bork, Cir. J., concurring), cert. denied, 471 U.S. 1127 (1985).

5. Robert H. Jackson, *The Supreme Court in the American System of Government* 56 (1955).

6. *Ollman*, 750 F.2d at 998 (Bork, Cir. J., concurring).

7. Ronald Dworkin's metaphor of the chain novel makes much the same point in a vivid and powerful fashion. See Dworkin, *Law's Empire* 228-38 (1986).

8. Richard Rorty, *Take Care of Freedom and Truth Will Take Care of Itself* 24 (Eduardo Mandieta ed., 2006).

9. See Phillip J. Cooper, *Battles on the Bench: Conflict Inside the Supreme Court* 57-63 (1995) (illustrating individual targeting and name calling in published opinions); David M. O'Brien, *Storm Center: The Supreme Court in American Politics* 275 (1986) (noting the increasing length of opinions); Richard A. Posner, *The Federal Courts: Crisis and Reform* 232-34 (1985) (describing the Court's tendency to employ abusive language); Bernard Schwartz, *Decision: How the Supreme Court Decides Cases* 48-55, 257-61 (1996) (discussing the delegation of opinion writing to clerks and the recycling of earlier opinions).

10. Joseph Goldstein, *The Intelligible Constitution* (1992).

11. On the distinction at issue, see Joseph Vining, *The Authoritative and the Authoritarian* (1986).

12. Chief Justice John Roberts's opinion for a unanimous Court (Justice Alito not participating) in *Rumsfeld v. Forum for Academic and Institutional Rights*, 547 U.S. 47 (2006) (upholding Congress's power to require law schools to permit military recruiters equal access to campus facilities despite the schools' objection to military policies concerning gay and lesbian personnel), can serve as a recent example of an opinion that substantially meets this need, although I suspect that Professor Goldstein might think it too long even so. The point, of course, is not whether Roberts reached the best constitutional conclusion, although the clarity of his opinion may well have something to do with the absence of dissent or even of any separate concurrences. Conscientious constitutional decision is not infallible; it is only the best that human beings who aren't angels can do.

13. See Wade H. McCree, Jr., Bureaucratic Justice: An Early Warning, 129 U. Pa. L. Rev. 777, 778 (1981), quoting Justice Brandeis as saying of the justices that "we do our own work." The comment exists in several slightly different versions, rather like Judge Hand's anecdote about Brandeis's friend Holmes.

14. In one of his books, Phillip Bobbitt appears to see the constitutional game in this light (or nearly so): he described the Constitution as morally agnostic "*vis-à-vis* individuals and their relationships in common" except with respect to its ban on slavery. See Bobbitt, *Constitutional Interpretation* 169 (1991).

15. Learned Hand, Chief Justice Stone's Concept of the Judicial Function (1946), in *The Spirit of Liberty* 204 (3d ed. 1960).

16. *United States v. Schwimmer*, 279 U.S. 644, 654 (1929) (Holmes, J., dissenting).

17. See, respectively, Wirt's opinion, Rights of Free Virginia Negroes, 1 Op. Att'y Gen. 506 (1821); *Scott v. Sandford*, 60 U.S. (19 How.) 393 (1857) (Taney, C.J.); *State v. Mann*, 13 N.C. (2 Dev.) 263 (1829) (Ruffin, J.); and Bates's opinion, Citizenship, 10 Op. Att'y Gen. 382 (1862). I analyze the Wirt and Bates opinions in H. Jefferson Powell, *A Community Built on Words* 171–77 (2002), and Ruffin's opinion in id. at 150–57.

18. 250 U.S. 616, 630 (1919) (Holmes, J., dissenting). It is interesting that Holmes wrote of the Constitution, not the First Amendment, as the experiment, although hardly surprising given his rejection in cases such as *Lochner v. United States* of any general attempt to claim the Constitution for a particular, contestable ideology.

CONCLUSION

1. See *Chisholm v. Georgia*, 2 U.S. (2 Dall.) 419 (1793). Justice James Iredell dissented, and the four justices in the majority all delivered separate ("seriatim") opinions. The executive announced the adoption of the amendment in January 1798, but in fact the requisite number of states had ratified Congress's proposal by February 1795. See 5 *Documentary History of the Supreme Court of the United States, 1789–1900* 627, 637–38 (Maeva Marcus ed., 1994).

2. Letter from Jay to Adams (Jan. 2, 1801), in 4 *The Correspondence and Public Papers of John Jay* 284, 285 (Henry P. Johnston ed., 1890).

3. There are, of course, other reasons for the rarity of Court-reversing amendments, among them the Court's willingness to reverse itself.

4. Abraham Lincoln, First Inaugural Address (Mar. 4, 1861), in 4 *Collected Works of Abraham Lincoln* 268 (Roy P. Basler ed., 1953). Recent

arguments for what is sometimes called popular constitutionalism include Mark Tushnet, *Taking the Constitution away from the Courts* (1999), and Larry D. Kramer, *The People Themselves: Popular Constitutionalism and Judicial Review* (2004).

5. Jay, in a hesitant but clear display of the constitutional virtue of candor, immediately noted the contradiction posed to his constitutional vision by slavery—Americans are joint sovereigns "without subjects (unless the African slaves among us may be so called)." On Jay's role in abolishing slavery in New York, see Roger G. Kennedy, *Burr, Hamilton, and Jefferson: A Study in Character* 89–105 (2000).

6. All the quotations from Jay's opinion, and his overall discussion of these themes, are found in 2 U.S. (2 Dall.) at 470–73 and 478–79. Justice James Wilson made a very similar argument. See id. at 454–56 (opinion of Wilson, J.).

INDEX